AF553316

SP
Pvt. Ltd.

This Book is Dedicated to

Our Brothers, Our Jawans Who Sacrificed Their Today for Our Tomorrow.

This Book is Also for all My Well Wishers

Who Helped Me to Let This Book Become a Reality.

Kashmir

Where Do We Go?

by

Samindra Mohan Biswas

2020

Studium Press (India) Pvt. Ltd.

Kashmir

Where Do We Go?

ISBN: 978-93-85046-65-0

Published by:

Studium Press (India) Pvt. Ltd.
4735/22, 2nd Floor, Prakash Deep Building
(Near Delhi Medical Association)
Ansari Road, Darya Ganj, New Delhi-110 002
Tel.: + 91-11-43240200-15 (15 lines); Fax: 91-11-43240215
E-mail: pubdir@studiumpress.in

Printed at India

ABOUT THE AUTHOR

Samindra Mohan Biswas studied at South Point School and Presidency College, now Presidency Univeraity, Kolkata and passed the M.A. Examination in Modern History from the University of Calcutta. He was awarded the Ph.D. degree in Arts on 20th August, 2007 by the University of Calcutta. His thesis was on the life and achievements of one of the most controversial characters and the first Prime Minister of undivided Bengal Abul Kasem Fazlul Huq which was published in book form in 2011. He has served as a guest lecturer in the Islamic Department of History and Culture, University of Calcutta and currently he is working as an Associate Professor in History at Bidhan Chandra College, Rishra, Hooghly, West Bengal.

PREFACE

Kashmir - Where Do We Go, was first presented in a seminar at Bidhan Chandra College, Rishra, Hooghly. From there it was decided to translate the discussion into a publication for which I am grateful and thankful to Studium Press for choosing me and giving me an opportunity to bring this burning topic to the readers as an appetizer. In this book I have tried to deviate from the traditional Kashmir problems and instead tried to show its history. Also as a change I have in this book tried to show how the rise of global and cross border terrorism has gradually gripped Kashmir. Also this book has tried to deal with the psyche of the Kashmiris and what ails them? As a cure for this ailment some solutions have been proposed. However, by the time this book is published every reader will be aware of the latest developments in Jammu and Kashmir including the abrogation of Article 35A and Article 370. Still, the relevancy will not be lost. As it has also tried to discuss the background and contents of Article 35A and Article 370 as well as the basis of Bilateral Relations regarding Kashmir *i.e.* The Shimla Agreement and before that The Tashkent Agreement. Also, the post abrogation Article 370 situation in Jammu and Kashmir has been highlighted. Further, the timeline of Indo-Pak Relations and the bilateral agreements have also been brought into focus. Moreover, how internal politics of the state has given rise to a policy of destruction have also been tried to be analysed. For this I am indebted to the newspaper offices and National Archives, New Delhi, National Library, Kolkata both its main and newspaper divisions.

TABLE OF CONTENTS

LIST OF FIGURES

INTRODUCTION

Kashmir, the name is such which instantly makes us to visualize a paradise, a valley of picturesque landscape, and fills our heart with awe and reverence. The beauty is such that once the Mughal emperor Shahjahan commented -

"If There Is Paradise On Earth It Is This,
It Is This, It Is This"
(Agar Firdaws Ba Roy, I Zamin Ast,
Hamin Ast-u, Hamin Ast-u, Hamin Ast-u)

SHAHJAHAN NAMA By Inayat Khan

Again, in the words of the famous Satyajit Ray, 'Bhuswarga Bhayankar') (Picture 1)

On the other hand, this paradise has witnessed since the ancient times till today the spilling of blood and the valley being sprewened with dead bodies due to the invasions by the Huns, the Sakas in the past and by the terrorists in recent times. However, the scenerio that is witnessed in recent times has not been so centuries ago though the Indian sub continent has been subjugated by the various intruders who invaded the Indian territory through the porous mountainous north western region the topography of which has not changed much even today. It is to be mentioned here that though we reference to Kashmir but Jammu and Kashmir together comprise the state of J & K, whereby Jammu I'd Hindu majority and Kashmir is muslim majority.

Having said the above, the history of Kashmir is quite an obvious, adorned with the names of some of the famous legendary figures, which we get from the only authentic written available source Kalhan's Rajtarangini. Coming to the sources that I have come across while studying the Kashmir problems, some of the important ones have been discussed here.

Kashmir is the northernmost geographical region of the subcontinent. Until the mid 19th century, Kashmir denoted only the Kashmir Valley between the Great Himalayas and the Pir Panjal Range.

Today, it denotes s larger area that includes the Indian Administered Territory of Jammu and Kashmir (which includes the divisions of Jammu & Kashmir Valley and Ladakh), the Pakistani administered territory of Azad Kashmir and Gilgit Baltistan and Chinese administered territory of Aksai Chin and the Trans Karakoram Tract.

In the first half of the first millennium, Kashmir was an important centre of Hinduism and later Buddhism and later still in the ninth century, Kashmir Shaivism arose. In 1339, Shah Mir became the first ruler of Kashmir, inaugurating Salatin-I-Kashmir or Shah Mir Dynasty. Kashmir became a part of the Mughal Empire from 1586 to 1751 and there after till 1820 under the Afghsn Durrani Empire. In the same year Ranjit Singh annexed Kashmir. In 1846, after the first defeat of the Sikhs in the first Anglo-Sikh War and upon the purchase of Kashmir from the British, Gulab Singh, the Raja of Jammu, became the new ruler of Kashmir. His successors ruled under the tutelage of the British until the Partition of India in 1947 when the former Princely State of the British Empire became a disputed region now administered by India, China and Pakistan.

While discussing Kashmir, one has to look into the position of the Muslims vis a vis the Hindus from the pre British days, across the British period till today. For this Joya Chatterjee's Bengal Divided (1932–47) and Ayesha Jalal's Jinnah - The Sole Spokesman, have provided the position of the Muslims as well as the role of

Picture 1: Kashmir Valley

Md. Ali Jinnah, in relation to the Congress leaders leading to the partition of India and the rise of the Kashmir problems.

In this context, the activities of the Indian Naional Congress and their position regarding the partition of India cannot remain untouched and in Dr. Sekhar Bandopadhyay, From Plassey To Partition and The Nationalist Movement in India, I have tried to look into their responses. Along with this, one cannot disregard Bengal as it was the nerve centre of political activities during the British period during which time, Abul Kasem Fazlul Huq, Sher-e-Bangla *i.e.* The Bengal Tiger, and his Krishak Praja Party played a leading role for the Bengali Muslim peasants. Moreover, in the company of Jinnah, he was instrumental in passing the Pakistan Resolution in the Lahore Congress in 1940, which subsequently led to the Great Calcutta Killing in 1946 and the partition of India in 1947. These aspects have been taken into account from two Bengali Books, Pakistan Prastab O Fazlul Huq by Amalendu De and Sukhoranjan Sengupta's Bangasanghar Ebong (1946–50).

It is said that today's Kashmir problem is a British legacy. The British could have put the dispute to rest permanently. To deal with this question, V.K. Menon's Tranfer of Power, two volumes of collection of British documents compiled in Edwards & Griffith ed. Documents of The Raj & Nicholas Mansergh's Transfer of Power (Vol. III–XII) have been consulted.

However, having analysed the above one of the most important personalities in the history of India *vis a vis* Kashmir and the first Prime Minister of independent India, Jawharlal Nehru cannot be left out of discussion. On the one hand, he was a close friend of the last viceroy of India, Lord Mountbatten and taking advantage of this relation Nehru was able to put the destiny in India's favour as far as the partition of India as well as Kashmir. His initial closeness with Sheikh Abdullah, who later became the Prime Minister of Kashmir as per article 35A and later Art. 370 hoped to settle Kashmir problem but later the separatist movement of the Kashmiris led by the Sheikh, supported by Pakistan since India and Pakistan became independent, the first Indo-Pak skirmish in 1947–48, the subsequent dismissal of Sheikh Abdullah and his government, Nehru's hasty decision of plebiscite and Nehru's hasty voluntary unilateral reference of Kashmir to the U.N.O. in 1960's have jeopardized the situation in Kashmir which is still continuing today. From A. Hingorani's Nehru's Foreign Policy and Jaswant Singh's India Independence these questions I have tried to look into.

It is from this time that the situation in Kashmir has begun to take a turn for the worse which is largely determined by Indo-Pak relations. The subsequent Indo-Pak Wars of 1965, 1970–71, the Kargil War of 1999 etc. have put the Kashmir situation in a tight spot. This brings us to the question of terrorism in Kashmir and its implications. It is to be remembered that terrorism in Indian perspective is nothing new. India have witnessed revolutionary terrorism during the British period in the struggle for independence in the 1920s & 1930s. However, with the passage of time and perspective the character of terrorism has also changed. Here, an attempt has been made to look into the different types of terrorism that has been affecting globally including India as well as to define terrorism. In this respect, Business Economy, pg. 38 (26th Aug. To 8th Sept.), 2006; Art. "Sleeping Over Security", B. Hoffman's Inside Terrorism, Columbia University Press have tried to delve into the matter under discussion.

From the above tentacles of terrorism, Kashmir also could not escape. Backed by Pakistan, coupled with the separatist tendencies of the Kashmiris, terrorism has totally gripped Kashmir. The situation is such that even the women folk and the students have taken anti-state stance. In this perspective, in the concluding chapter, an effort has been put to find some probable solutions to this seemingly unending problem.

Having said the above and after studying the above references and books, however, a satisfactory analysis of Kashmir problems, covering its ancient history to the modern times and post abrogation of Article 370 situation has not been looked into. So I have tried in this book to analyze and delve into the question what ails Kashmir and what is the position of Kashmir aftermath the abrogation of Article 370.

In Chapter I the History of Kasmir and the genealogy of the Kashmir kings have been discussed. Here, an effort has been made to study the Hindu rulers of Kashmir from the times of the Mahabharata till the rule of the Dogra rulers, which ends with Raja Hari Singh. To be noted at that time the population of Kashmir was Hindu. It was only after the Muslim invasion in the 9th century that the muslims began to settle there as the invasions took place through the porous north western frontier region.

Chapter II discusses the events leading to the partition of India and its effects.

In this chapter the change over of administrative set up from the Mughals to the British, the change of the psyche of the relatively peace loving subjects into anti-British attitude due to the British policy of Divide and Rule, the rise of Sir Syed Ahmed Khan and his advocacy for special treatment of the muslims for their backwardness in relation to the Hindus as well as the demographic changes in India along with the birth and roles of the Muslim League and Indian National Congress *vis a vis* the growth of communalism and partition of India have been discussed.

Chapter III has tried to highlight the post partition scenerio, the role of Raja Hari Singh in acceding to India and his attitude regarding Kashmir, the role of Nehru and Sheikh Abdullah towards Kashmir and their relationship. Also, Art. 35A and Art. 370, the rise of Shekh Abdullah as a separatist leader, his subsequent dismissal from the post of Prime Ministership of Kashmir, his arrest, the dissolution of J & K Legislative Assembly, Nehru's unilateral decision of plebiscite and referring the Kashmir issue to the U.N.O. have been highlighted here.

Chapter IV analyses the Indo-Pak relations arising out of Indo-Pak wars since 1947 till date and its effect on J & K. as well as the continuous tendencies of Pakistan to destabilize the state of J & K by abating and supporting cross border terrorism.

Chapter V looks into the aspect of the rise of global terrorism and its implications on the world including India and Jammu & Kashmir. In this context an attempt has been made to define terrorism and their characters, to analyze how the states are responsible for their rise and abating terrorism as well as the sincerity of the government to counter this by taking proper action without any political gimmick; how the Kashmiris due to the lack of development of economy, have fallen prey to terrorism, which initially though was at a low level but gradually it is becoming out of bounds; more alarming is the way the girl students, the women and the young generation is taking to terrorism and anti state activities.

Chapter VI deals with aspect of the rise of various global terrorist outfits and their influence on the separatist activities in J & K and their sponsors that are operating both inside and cross border.

Chapter VII has tried to analyze the question Kashmir- Where Do We Go? Here, we will be trying to see how terrorism has affected India right from Mumbai blast in 1990s till the Pulwama attack and Balakot strike; not only this the way the government is losing mass contact especially in Kashmir is perplexing us; in this context we will see how the Kashmiris are turning away from helping the government which was not the case in Kargil, 1999. And if this continues there is a chance of a serious consequence which may not augur well not only for the subcontinent but for the world as well.

In Chapter VIII an attempt has been made to find some solutions depending on the sincerity and responses of the government without any prejudice. This solution is directed both at the political and military level as well as at the mass level.

The last Chapter looks into the scenario post abrogation of Article 370 and tries to analyze its future.

In the concluding chapter an overall assessment has been made in my endeavor to search for peace. It is true that the way terrorism is devouring even the children of the educated as well as affluent classes it is very difficult to get rid of this disease easily. But trust of the masses in the government and vice versa can do away with the vices in the long run and forth is social and economic upliftment is the only solution.

1

HISTORY OF KASHMIR

Kashmir is one name which once filled one's heart with an imagination of gateway to Heaven. But with the progress of time the imagination and definition also changed. Heaven has now turned into Hell as Kashmir today has become synonymous with terror. It is such that if anyone wants to commit suicide Kashmir is the perfect place. Still a a student of History, the origin of the name of Kashmir needs to be examined.

The name Kashmir, paradise on earth, is derived from the Sanskrit word Kasmira. According to Nilamata Purana, Ka means water and Shimir means to dedicate. Hence, Kashmir stands for a land dedicated from water. Further, the Nilmata Purana gives the name Kashmiri, considering it to be an embodiment of Uma. It also stated that Kashmir was born from a lake known as Sati Saras. In the Rajtarangini, a history of Kashmir witten by Kalhana in the 12th century, it is stated that the valley of Kashmir was formerly a lake. It is said that a great sage or rishi Kashyapa drained it by cutting a gap in the hills at Baramullah. When water was drained out of Kashmir, Kashyapa asked the Brahmans to settle there. (Picture 2) Because it was due to Kashyapa that a settlement was developed, the region where the settlement grew was known as Kasyapura.[1] So alternatively, Kashmir could have derived its

[1] Christopher Snedden-Understanding Kashmir and the Kashmiris, Oxford University Press, p. 22, Wikipedia.

name from Kashyapa Mir *i.e.* Kashyapa's Lake or Kashyapa Meru *i.e.* Kashyapa's Mountain.[2]

Interestingly, the word Kashmir has been referred to in a Hindu scripture mantra worshiping the Hindu Goddess Sharada, which again might have been in reference to the place of Hindu worship, Sharada Peeth.[3]

The ancient Greeks called the region Kasperia, which has been identified with Kaspapyros, of Hecataeus of Miletus (or Stephanus of Byzantium). Kashmir is also believed to be the country meant by Ptolemy's Kaspeiria.[4]

The earliest text which directly mentions the name Kashmir is in Astadhyayi written by a Sanskrit Grammarian, Panini in the 5th century B.C. Panini called the people of Kashmir as Kashmirikas.[5]

Some earlier references of Kashmir can also be found in the Sabha Parva of the Mahabharata and in Puranas like Matsya Purana, Vayu Purana, Padma Purana and Vishnu Purana as well as Vishnudharmottara Purana.[6]

Hiuentsang, the Buddhist scholar and Chinese traveller called Kashmir as Kia-shi-milo, while some other Chinese accounts referred Kashmir as ki-pin and ache-pin. In the Kashmiri language, Kashmir itself is known as Kasheer.[7]

---

2 Ibid.

3 Ibid.

4 Suhail Khan-Who Killed Kasheer, Notion Press, Wikipedia.

5 Braja Bihari Kumar-India and Central Asia, From Classical To Contemporary Period, Concept Publishing Company, p. 64. Also, Mohini Qasba Raina-Kashur, The Kashmiri Speaking People, Partridge Publishing, Singapore, p. 11, Wikipedia.

6 Kulbhusan-Cultural Heritage of Kashmiri Pandits, Pentagon Press, pp. 2–3, Wikipedia.

7 Mohini Qasba Raina-Kashur The Kashmiri speaking people, Partridge Publishing, Singapore, p. 11, Wikipedia.

During the ancient and medieval period, Kashmir has been an important centre for the development of Hindu-Buddhist syncretism, in which Madhyamaka and Yogachara were blended with Shaivism and Advaita Vedanta. Mauryan emperor, Ashoka, who took to Buddhism after the Kalinga War in 261 B.C., is often credited with having founded the old capital of-Kashmir, Shrinagari, today lying on the outskirts of modern Srinagar. Interestingly, Kashmir is to be the stronghold of Buddhism. As a Buddhist seat of learning, the Sarvastivad school of learning strongly influenced Kashmir.[8]

East and Central Asian Buddhist monks are recorded as having visited the kingdom. In the late 4th century A.D. the famous Kuchanese monk, Kumarajiva, born to an Indian noble family, Dirghagama and Madhyagama in Kashmir under Bandhudatta. Another Buddhist monk Vimalaksa, a Sarvastivadan Buddhist monk, traveled from Kashmir to Kucha and there instructed Kumarajiva in the Vinayapitaka.[9]

If we look at the history of the rulers of Kashmir, then the earliest ruler that we get is Gonanda (3238–3188 B.C.). The history of Kashmir is recorded since 3450 B.C. through Rajtarangini written by Kalhana. Kashmir has more than 5400 years of history. During the Mahabharata era, Kambojas ruled Kashmir with a Republican system of government from the capital city of Karna-Rajapuram-Gatva Kamboja-Nirjitastava shortened to Rajapura, which is modern Rajauri. Peer Panjal, which is part of modern Kashmir is a witness to this fact. To be noted that Panjal is a simply distorted form of the Sanskritic tribal term Panchala. Muslims prefixed the word peer to it in memory of Siddha Faqir and the name thereafter changed to Peer Panjal.[10]

In fact, Jammu was founded by Hindu King Raja Jambu Lochan in the 14th century B.C. During one of his hunting campaigns he reached the Tawi river where he saw a goat and a lion were

[8] A. K. Warder-Indian Buddhism, Motilal Banarsidass, pp. 263–264.

[9] P. Ram-Life In India.

[10] Kalhan's Rajtarangini, www.booksfact.com

drinking water at the same place. The king was impressed and decided to set up a town after his name, Jamboo. With the passage of time the name became corrupted and came to be known as Jammu.[11]

Kalhan's Rajtarangini has all the 8000 sanskrit verses which were completed by 1150 B.C. and chronicles the history of Kashmir dynasty from Mahabharat times to 12th century *i.e.* 4600 years of history and the complete list of Kashmir's kings.[12]

In fact, Gonanda I was a relative of Magadh ruler Jarasandha and contemporary to Yudhistir. He was killed by Lord Krishna's elder brother Balaram. His son Damodar I was killed by Lord Krishna.[13] Later, Lord Krishna made his wife Yasovati temporary ruler for six months, who was succeeded by her son Gonanda II. He was killed in a battle with Parikshit, grandson of Arjun and King of Hastinapur in 3083 B.C. As Gonanda has no heir, Parikshit took over the Kingdom of Kashmir, incorporated into his empire and handed it over to Harnadev, who was from his family. From Harnadev, the Pandav dynasty ruled over Kashmir for 1331 years from 3083–1752 B.C.[14]

Next in line of succession in the dynasty of Gonanda I was Asoka or Dharmasoka. Gonanda I was a poet. Dharmasoka, who belonged to the Gonanda dynasty and was also a poet, freed himself from sins by embracing Buddhism and built the city of Srinagar, with ninety-six lakhs of houses resplendent with wealth. Asoka or Dharmasoka ruled from 1448–1440 B.C. He lost his kingdom as the Mlechhas occupied it and he fled to the forest. Later his son Jaelauka reconqured it. Jaelauka ruled from 1400–1344 B.C. He was succeeded by Damodara II (1344–1294 B.C.), Hushka, Jushka and Kanishka (2294–1234 B.C.), and Abhimanyu (1234–1182 B.C.).[15]

---

[11] Ibid.

[12] Ibid.

[13] Ibid.

[14] Kalhan's Rajtarangini, www.booksfact.com

[15] Ibid.

The dynasty of Gonanda reappeared when Gonanda III took over the reigns in in 1182 B.C. and ruled till 1147 B.C. He was succeeded by Vibhishana (1147–1092 1/2 B.C.), Indrajit (1092 1/2–1057 B.C.), Ravana (1057–1027 B.C.), Vibhishana II (1027–991 1/2 B.C.), Kinnara or Nara (991 1/2–952 B.C.), Siddha (952–892 B.C.), Utpslaksha (892–861 1/2 B.C.), Hiranyaksha (861 1/2–824 B.C.), Hiranyakula (824–764 B.C.), Vasukula (764–704 B.C.), Mihirkula (704–634 B.C.), Baka (934–594 B.C.), Kshitinamdana (594–564 B.C.), Vasunamdana (564–512 B.C.). Vasunamdana was a poet and author of Samara Sastra. He was succeeded by Nara (512–477 B.C.), Aksha (477–417 B.C.,), Gopaditya (417–357 B.C.), This Gopaditya built the temple of Adi Sankara in 367–366 B.C. He founded several temples and Agraharams. He was also a poet. He was succeeded by Gokarna (357–322 B.C.). He was succeeded by Kinkhila or Narendraditya (322–285 B.C.).He was succeeded by Andha Yudhistir, who ruled from 285–272 B.C. (He was called so by the people for his small eyes. But he was not blind).[16]

The dynasty of Pratapaditya ruled from 272–80 B.C. with a total of six kings, the last king in the line being Sandhimati (127–80 B.C.) This Pratapaditya who ruled from 272–240 B.C.) was the 74th king of Kashmir and as mentioned in the Rajtarangini as a relative of Vikramaditya was brought by the ministers from a distant land and placed on the throne of Kashmir. Interestingly, Vikramaditya referred to here might be Sri Harsha Vikramaditya of Ujjain, who ruled from 457 B.C. However, Kalhan says that this Vikramaditya, the relative of Pratapaditya, was not the Sakari Vikramaditya from 57 B.C.[17]

Sandhimati was succeeded by Meghavahana (80–46 B.C.), Pravarsena or Sreshtasena or Tunjina (46–16 B.C.), and Hiranya (16 B.B.–14 C.E.). This Hiranya died useless and was the elder brother of Toramana, the Huna leader, who with his wife and son were in exile. Hiranya was succeeded by Matrigupta (14 C.E.–19 C.E.). He was sent by Emperor Vikramaditya of Ujjain as King of

[16] Ibid.

[17] Kalhan's Rajtarangini, www.booksfact.com

Kashmir. He was succeeded by Pravarasena II (Toramana's son, 19–79 C.E.), and Yudhistira II (79–118 C.E.). This Yudhistira was contemporary to Salivahana, who was the founder of Era 78 C.E. He was succeeded by Lakshmana (Narendraditya–118–131 C.E.), Tunjina or Ranaditya (Poet–131–173 C.E.), Vikramaditya (173–215 C.E.) and Baladitya (215–252 C.E.).[18]

The next dynasty that came to rule over Kashmir was the Karkota Dynasty with Durlabha Vardhana (son in law of Baladitya) taking over the reigns. The last king of this dynasty being Sukhvarma (845–852 C.E.). A total of seventeen kings of this dynasty ruled over Kashmir for 600 years.[19]

In the eighth century, the Karkota established themselves as the rulers of Kashmir. Kashmir grew as an imperial power under the Karkotas. Chandrapida of this dynasty was recognized as by an Imperial order of the Chinese Emperor as the King of Kashmir. His successor Lalitaditya Muktapida led a successful military campaign against the Tibetans. He then defeated Yasshovarman of Kanyakubja and subsequently conquered eastern kingdoms of Magadh, Kamrupa, Gauda and Kalinga. Lalitaditya extended his influence over Malwa and Gujarat and defeated the Arabs at Sindh.[19A] After his demise Kashmir's influence over other kingdoms declined and the dynasty ended in 855–856 C.E.[19B]

Karkota Empire was a powerful Hindu empire which originated in the region of Kashmir around 625 C.E. It's founder was Durlabhvardhana around the time of Harsha.[20]

The dynasty marked the rise of Kashmir as a power in South Asia.[21] Avanti Varma ascended the throne of Kashmir in 855 C.E. establishing the Utpala Dynasty and ending the rule of Karkota

---

[18] Ibid.

[19] Ibid.

[19A] R. C. Majumdar- Advanced History of India, 1977, pp. 260–263.

[19B] Singh, 2008, pp. 571.20. P. Ram-Life In India, Wikipedia.

[20] Kalhan's Rajtarangini, www.booksfact.com.

[21] Ibid.

Dynasty.[22] To be noted that Lalitaditya or Mukatapida, a poet and ruler of Karkota dynasty who ruled Kashmir from 431–467 C.E. built the famous Martanda Temple (Sun Temple) in Kashmir.

Avantivarma who founded the Utpala dynasty in 855 C.E. ruled upto 880 C.E. In his court flourished many poets like Anandavardhana, Ratnakar etc. In fact a total of eight kings of this dynasty ruled for 84 years.[23]

Political instability in the 10th century made the royal body guards (Tantrins) very powerful in Kashmir. Under the Tantrins civil administration collapsed and chaos reigned in Kashmir till they were defeated by Chakravarnan.[23A] Queen Didda, who descended from the Hindu Shahis of Kabul on her mother's side, took over as the ruler in the second half of the 10th century.[23B]

Meanwhile, in 995 C.E., Yasaskara, who ruled from 936 C.E. and continued upto 945 1/2 C.E. founded the Gupta Brahmin rule in Kashmir. He was succeeded by, Varnata (1 month), Sangramadeva (5 months 945–946 C.E.), Parvagupta (946–948 C.E.), Kshemagupta (948–957 C.E.), and Abhmanyugupta (957–971 C.E.). To be noted that Abhimanyugupta was a minor, ruled by mother Didda or Diththa Devi, wife of Kshemagupta. Didda was contemporary to Bhima Shahi of Kabul, descendant of Lalya Shahi. Didda was a grand daughter of Bhima Shahi and daughter of Simharaja of Lohar dynasty.[24] Next successors were–Nandigupta (second son of Didda, 971–972 C.E.),

Tribhuvanagupta (third son of Didda, 972–974 C.E.), and Bhimsgupta (4th son of Didda, 974–979 C.E.). Since all sons were minors, so their mother Didda became regent and ruled on their behalf. Didda herself ruled from 979–1012 C.E.).[25]

---

[22] Sailendra Nath Sen-Ancient Indian History and Civilization, New Age International, p. 295.

[23] Kalhan's Rajtarangini, www.booksfact.com.

[23A] Majumdar, Advanced History of India, 1977, p. 357.

[23B] Singh, 2008, p. 571.

[24] Ibid.

[25] Kalhan's Rajtarangini, www.booksfact.com.

Simharaja, also son-in-law of Bhima Shahi of Kabul of Thomara dynasty, founded the Lohar dynasty. However, the ten Brahmin kings of the Gupta Brahmin dynasty ruled for 76 years.[26]

Sangramraja, who founded the Lohar dynasty and ruled from 1076 to 1027 C.E., was a brother's son of Didda,and contemporary to Trilochana of Pal of Kabul. Next was Hariraja who ruled for 22 days only. After him, Anantadeva ruled from 1027–1062 and 1062–1078. Anantadeva was dethroned for a few days in 1062 but came back. Next, Kalasa or Ranaditya (Pandit and poet ruled from 1078–1088 C.E.), Utkarsha (ruled for a few days), and Harsha (1088–1110 C.E.). A total of six kings belonging to Lohar dynasty ruled for 98 years.[27]

Next came Uchchla, who ruled for a few days and found the Agni Vamsa or Brahman Kshatriya dynast in Kashmir. Then came Sanjaraja (1110–1120 C.E.), Sussals (1120–1128 C.E.) and Jayasimha (1228–1148 C.E.). The author if Rajtarangini, Kalhan's time was 1148 C.E. His father was a tributary to the King of Kashmir besides being a Prime Minister. This family might have been a branch of the Satavahana dynasty.[28]

Lohar dynasty paved the way for the foreign invasion Kashmir. Suhadeva, the last king of the Lohar dynasty fled Kashmir after Zulju (Dulacha), a Turkish Mongal chief laid a savage raid in Kashmir. Rinchana, a Tibetan Buddhist refugee established himself as the ruler of Kashmir after Zulju. Rinchana's conversion to Islam is a Kashmiri folklore. He was persuaded to accept Islam by his minister Shah Mir, probably for political reasons. From the 14th century Islam gradually became a dominant religion in Kashmir.[29]

Before Shamsuddin Shah Mir took over the reigns of Kashmir, Queen Kota Rani, was a medieval Hindu ruler of Kashmir, who

---

[26] Ibid.

[27] Ibid.

[28] Ibid.

[29] Ibid.

ruled till 1339. She was often credited with saving the city of Srinagar from recurring flood by getting a canal constructed, which was named after her "Kutte Kol". This canal receives water from River Jhelum at the entry point of the city and again merges with the river beyond city limits.[30]

Shamsuddin Shah Mir (1339–1342), was the first Muslim ruler of Kashmir and founder of the Shah Mir dynasty.[31] Kashmiri historian Jonaraja in his Dvitiya Rajtarangini mentioned Shah Mir was from the country of Panchagahvara (identified as the Panjgabbar valley between Rajauri and Budhal, an area situated to the south of Divasagar Pargana in the valley of River Abs, a tributary of Chenab.) and his ancestors were kshatriyas who converted to Islam.[32]

Scholar A. Q. Rafiqi stated that Shah Mir arrived in Kashmir in 1313 along with his family during the reign of Suhadeva (1301–20), whose service he entered. In subsequent years, through his tact and ability, Shah Mir rose to prominence and became one of the important personalities of the time. Later after the death of Udayanadeva, the brother of Suhadeva, he was able to assume the kingship himself and thus laid the foundation of a permanent Muslim rule in Kashmir. Dissension among the ruling classes and foreign invasions were the two main factors which contributed towards the establishment of Muslim rule in Kashmir.[33]

Muslim Ulema such as Mir Sayyid Ali Hamadani, arrived from Central Asia to proselytize in Kashmir and their efforts converted

---

[30] Prithvi Nath Kaul Bamzai-Culture and Political History of Kashmir, M. D. Publications Pvt. Ltd., Wikipedia.

[31] Carlos Ramirez Faria-Concise Encyclopedia of World History, 412, Wikipedia.

[32] R. S. Sharma-A Comprehensive History of India, Orient Longman, p. 628. Also, N. K. Zutshi-Sultan Zain-ul-Abidin of Kashmir, An Age Of Enlightenment, Nupur Prakasgan, pp. 6–7.

[33] N. A. Baloch, A. Q. Rafiqi-The regions of Sind, Balochistan, Multan and Kashmir, in M. S. Asimov, C. E. Bosworth (*Eds.*)-History of Civilization of Central Asia, Volume IV, Part I-The Age of Achievement: A. D. 750 to the end of the 15th century- the historical, social and economic setting, UNESCO, pp. 297–322, Wikipedia.

thousands of Kashmiris to Islam.[34] In fact, a large number of Muslim Ulema came from Central Asia to Kashmir to preach; Sayyid Bilal Sgah, Sayyid Jalaluddin of Bukhara, Sayyid Tajuddin, his brother Sayyid Husayn Simani, Sayyid Ali Hamadani, Shaykh Nuruddin were some of the well known ulama who played a significant role in spreading Islam in Kashmir.[35]

By the late 1400s most Kashmiris had accepted Islam. Persian was introduced in Kashmir by the Shah Miri Dynasty (1349–1561) and started to flourish under Sultan Zany-al-Abedin (1420–70).[36]

The Mughal emperor Akbar conquered Kashmir from 1585–86 taking advantage of Kashmir's internal Shia-Sunni divisions and thus ended indigenous Kashmiri Muslim rule.[37] Akbar added it to the Kabul Subah (encompassing modern day Afghanistan, northern Pakistan, and the Kashmir valley of India) but Shah Jahan carved it out as a separate subah with its seat at Srinagar. Kashmir became the northern most region of Mughal India, as well as a pleasure ground in the summer time. They built Persian water-gardens in Srinagar, along the shores of Dal Lake, with cool and elegantly proportioned terraces, fountains, roses, jasmine and rows of chinar trees.[38]

The Afghan Durrani dynasty's Durrani Empire from 1751, when a weak 15th Mughal emperor Ahmed Shah's Bahadur's Viceroy Muin-ul-Mulk was defeated and reinstated by the Durrani founder Ahmed Shah Durrani (who conquered roughly modern day Afghanistan and Pakistan from the Mughals and local rulers) until the 1820 Sikh triumph. The Afghan rulers brutally repressed Kashmiris of all faiths.[39]

---

[34] Tahir Amin, Victoria Schofield-Kashmir, The Oxford Encyclopedia of the Islamic World, Wikipedia.

[35] Ibid.

[36] Encyclopedica Iranica-Kashmir, Wikipedia.

[37] Christopher Snedden-Understanding Kashmir and Kashmiris, Oxford University Press, p. 29. Also, Balraj Puri-5000 years of Kashmir, pp. 43–45, Wikipedia.

[38] Isabel Hilton-Betwen the mountains, Wikipedia.

[39] Chitralekha Zutshi-Languages of Belonging: Islam, Regional Identity, and the making of Kashmir, C. Hurst & Co. Publishers, p. 35.

In 1819, the rule of the Kashmir valley changed hands from those of the Afghan Durrani Empire to the invading armies of Ranjit Singh of the Punjab, thus ending four centuries of Muslim rule under the Mughals and the Afghan regime. Because of the sufferings of the Kashmiris at the hands of the Afghan rulers, they initially welcomed the new Sikh rulers.[40] However, the Sikh governors turned out to be hardtaskmasters, while Sikh rule was generally considered oppressive, the Kashmiris were perhaps protected by the remoteness of Kashmir from the capital of the Sikh empire in Lahore.[41]

The Sikh rulers passed a number of aanti Muslim laws which included handing out death sentences for cow slaughter, closing down of Jama Masjid in Srinagar, and banning the Afghan, the public Muslim call to prayer.[42]

A number of European visitors who visited Kashmir at that time wrote of abject poverty of the vast Muslim peasantry which might again be due to the exorbitant taxes imposed by the Sikhs. This according to some contemporary accounts resulted in the depopulation of a large tract of land in the countryside allowing only one-sixth of the land to be cultivated as many had migrated to the plains of the Punjab.[43]

However, after a famine in 1832, the Sikhs reduced the land tax to half the produce of the land and also began to offer interest free loans to the farmers. During this time Kashmiri shawls became famous worldwide, attracting customers especially from the west.[44]

The state of Jammu which has been on the ascendancy after the fall of the Mughal Empire, came under the control of the Sikhs

[40] Schofield-Kashmir in Conflict, pp. 5-6.

[41] Madan-Kashmir, Kashmiris, Kashmiriyat, p. 15. Also, Zutshi-Language of Belonging, pp. 39–41.

[42] Ibid.

[43] Ibid. Also, Chitralekha Zutshi-Languages of Belonging: Islam, Regions Identity and the Making of Kashmir, C. Hurst & Co. Publishers, p. 40.

[44] Ibid.

in 1770. Further in 1808, it was fully conquered by Maharaja Ranjit Singh. Gulab Singh, then a youngster in the House of Jammu, enrolled in the Sikh troops and by distinguishing himself in campaigns, gradually resee in power and influence. In 1822 , he was anointed as the Raja of Jammu.[45] Along with his able General Zorawar Singh Kahluria, he conquered and subdued Rajaouri (1821), Kishtawar (1821), Suru Valley and Kargil (1835), Ladakh (1834–40) and Baltistan (1840), thereby surrounding the Kashmir valley.[46]

In 1845, the first Anglo-Sikh War occurred. According to the Imperial Gazetteer of India, "Gulab Singh contrived to hold himself till the Battle of Sobraon, when he appeared as a useful mediator and a trusted advisor of Sir Henry Lawrence. Two treaties were concluded. By the first, the state of Lahore *i.e.* West Punjab was handed over to the British, as equivalent for one crore indemnity, the hill countries between the rivers Beas and Indus. By the second the British made over to Gulab Singh for 75 lakhs all the hilly and mountainous country situated to the east of the Indus and the west of the Ravi *i.e.* the vale of Kashmir.[47]

Drafted by a treaty and a bill of sale and constituted between 1820 and 1858, the Princely Sate of Kashmir and Jammu (as it was first called) combined disparate regions, religion and ethnicity. To the east, Ladakh was ethnically and culturally Tibetan and it's inhabitants practised Buddhism. To the south, Jammu had a mixed population of Hindus, Muslims and Sikhs., in the highly located Cental Kashmir valley, where the population were overwhelmingly Sunni Muslim, however, there was a small but influential Hindu minority *i.e.* the Kashmiri Brahmins or pandits; to the north east sparsely populated Baltistan had a population ethnically related to Ladakh but which practised Shia Islam; to the north also sparsely populated, Gilgit Agency, was an area of diverse, mostly Shia groups; and to the west, Punch was Muslim, but of different

[45] K. M. Panikkar: pp. 10–11, 14–34.

[46] Schofield-Kashmir in Conflict, pp. 6–7.

[47] Imperial Gazetteer of India, 'Kashmir History', Volume 15, pp. 94–95.

ethnicity than the Kashmir valley.[48] After the revolt of 1857, where Kashmir sided with the British, and the subsequent assumption of direct rule by Great Britain, the princely state of Kashmir came under the hegemony of the British Crown.

In the British census of India, 1941 Kashmir registered a Muslim majority population of 77%, a Hindu population of 20%, and a sparse population of the Buddhists and Sikhs comprising the remaining 3%.[49] That same year, Prem Nath Bazaaz, a Kashmiri Pandit journalist wrote: "The poverty of the Muslim masses were appalling ...Most are landless labourers, working as serfs for absentee (Hindu) landlords...Almost the whole brunt of official corruption is borne by the Muslim masses.[50] Under the Hindu rule, Muslims faced hefty taxation, discrimination in the legal system and were forced into labour without any wages.[51]

Conditions in the princely state caused a significant migration of people from the Kashmir valley to the Punjab of British India.[52] For almost a century until the census, a small Hindu elite had ruled over a vast and impoverished Muslim peasantry.[53]

Driven into docility by chronic indebtedness to the landlords and moneylenders, having no education, nor any awareness of rights the Muslim peasantry had no political representation until the 1930s.[54]

---

[48] Paul Browser-Kashmir, Research Paper, Wikipedia.

[49] Sumantra Bose-Roots of Conflict, Path to Peace, pp. 15–17.

[50] Ibid.

[51] Tahir Amin, Victoria Schofield-Kashmir, The Oxford Encyclopedia of the Islamic World, Wikipedia.

[52] Sumatra Bose-Transforming India, Harvard University Press, p. 211.

[53] Ibid.

[54] Ibid.

2

THE ROAD TO PARTITION

The demographic conditions that has been discussed in the previous chapter in relation to Kashmir, where it has been found that the Muslims constituted the majority population especially in Kashmir is a reflection of the same regarding the Indian subcontinent as a whole. This is due to the high birth rate of the Muslims which is considered to be high, the conversions and the influx of population across the border. Again, the present demographic scenerio is a replica of the past that led to the partition of India in 1947. Turning back to the days of the Islamic rule in India that is both during the Sultanate and the Mughal periods, *i.e.* almost six hundred years of Muslim rule saw the Muslims in the driving seat though Hindus were also accommodated in the administrative set up especially during the reign of Akbar. However, the last days of rule by Aurangzeb witnessed anti Muslim sentiment on the rise among the non Muslim sections of the populace. This led to sporadic revolts like agrarian revolts, Sikh revolts and clashes with the Marathas in the 18th century when the Mughal rule was on the decline and the regional powers tried to assert their independence. It must be admitted that though the Hindus were subjects of the Muslim rulers never throughout the six decades of the Muslim rule Hindu Muslim tension or communalism appeared in the scene. The relation was that of a master and a subject. The ideas derived from Islamic history and thought, both in terms of practical and doctrinal considerations, have influenced the behavior of the Muslims throughout the world. But these inflow of thoughts have been tampered by interactions with local cultures and value systems giving rise to new syncretism and eclectic systems of thought as well as cultural patterns.[1]

The decline of the Mughal empire saw the arrival of the foreign powers like English East India Co., The French East India Co., the Dutch, and the Portuguese jumping into the fray for flexing their muscles in the Indian subcontinent as regards to controlling political authority and in this context the main players were the French and the English. The vast amount of wealth hiding in the green fields of Bengal in the 18th century and the huge opportunity that was associated with it coupled with lack of any stable centralized political authority had opened a vast sea of opportunities whose call could not be ignored by the neo imperialists. Among the private players who joined the fray the French and the English East India Companies emerged as the two powerful contenders though at the end of three Carnatic wars fought between 1740s and 1760s the English East India Co. came out as the sole leader. It is to be mentioned here that in 1757, the Battle of Plassey and the 1765 Battle of Buxar had already decided the fate of Bengal. Therefore, the transition of English East India Co. from a private trading company to a colonial ruler and the change of administrative set up from Islamic Rule to Western Administraton opened up a new era in the history of India.

The previous chapter has discussed the past history of Kashmir which also saw how the Muslims have been subjugated by the dominant Hindus and others. Also, due to the high birth rate of the Muslims, the Muslim invasion, the conversions and the influx from across the border resulted in the increase of population not only in Kashmir proper but also throughout the Indian subcontinent in the 18th and 19th centuries. This rising Muslim population ultimately had an adverse impact on the politico-socio-economic-religious conditions of India.

[1] Tazeen M. Murshid-The Sacred and The Secular, p. 1.

However, the six centuries of Muslim rule from the foundation of the Sultanate period till the decline of the Mughal administration told a different story. It was true that the Hindus, who formed the majority populace of the subcontinent had been subjugated by the Muslim conquerors still they were never left ignored. This may be due to the fact that the Mughals especially made India their homeland unlike the British. Babur himself had been a fugitive after he was driven out of his birthplace after his father's death, by his uncle Uzbek, Shaibani Khan from his homeland at Farghana. As he roamed about like a pawn on a chess board in search of a living place, an invitation to invade the Indian subcontinent from the then Governor of the Punjab, Daulat Khan Lodi made Babur jump in joy. This coupled with the story of treasure that is hidden here and which he had dreamt of from his childhood lured Babur to come to India and settle here permanently. So the Mughals despite being of Turko-Mongol origin Indianised themselves and made India their homeland which is reflected in their administration.[1A]

The ideas derived from Islamic History and thought both in terms of practical and doctrinal considerations, have influenced the behaviour of the Muslims throughout the world. But these inflow of thoughts have been tempered by interaction with local cultures and value systems of thought as well as cultural patterns.[2]

Hence, there was no disharmony between the Hindus and the Muslims despite the Muslims being at the helm of affairs. The hindus were accommodated and trusted in the administration and sometimes even more than their counterparts. The last days of the rule of Aurangzeb saw a different picture.

Due to Aurangzeb's failure in stabilizing the economy and the political conditions and his distrust of his subjects coupled with his religious bigotry, antagonism began to emerge against the central authority. The resultant revolts and protests by different

---

[1A] R. C. Majumdar (ed.)-Advanced History of India, Conclusion.
[2] Tazeen M. Murshid-The Sacred and The Secular, p. 1.

communities made it very difficult for Araungazeb to rule. Still, after the death of Aurangzeb in 1707, the Mughal empire survived till 1857 amidst parties and politics in Mughal court. And ultimately, it was because of the weak rulers and economic degeneration that the six centuries of Muslim rule met its end paving a way for the rise of a new power unknown to India.[3]

The degeneration of the Mughal empire witnessed a change in the socio-political scenerio of India when the English East India Company began to make dents into Indian administrative sphere. Besides, this century witnessed the rise of some local powerful states on the ruins of the Mughal empire.[4]

Therefore, taking advantage of the political crisis in India aftermath the decline of the Mughal empire, the English East India Co. became engaged in transforming the Indian subcontinent into a colony of London Government. Along with the political expansion of the English Company, they were also involved in commercial expansion.[5]

Once Gallaghe and Robinson taking into account the consistent performance of the English in the history of Britsh imperialism, commented that the British policy was if possible then they should continue with trading while maintaining indirect control over their area of domination, however, where needed they should rule in the interest of their trade.[6] In fact, the English East India Co. ensured earning profit through indirect rule But sometimes the method of earning revenue required direct rule. At the same time the private trade of the English East India Co. resulted in the flourishing of private traders and the expansion of priivate trade as well.[7]

Again, from the trading activities there arose the desire for occupation of lands. The political instability in the subcontinent

[3] Satish Chandra-The Parties and Politics in Mughal Court; Introduction.
[4] Sekhar Bandopadhyay-From Plassey To Partition; Introduction.
[5] Ibid.
[6] Ibid, p. 71.
[7] Ibid.

and lack of unity increased the appetite for conquests. It is to be mentioned that despite the decline of the Mughal empire the local princely kingdoms had remained powerful though their armies and organizations remained inferior to these of the British. In this context, Keynes and Hopkins commented that these local princely states had a hand behind the rise of the English East India Co. as an administrative power. An entente developed between the Indian princes and the British centering around the land and money on England. From this the English formed an idea that real power was vested on the land. And that was the reason the English in order to maintain their commercial activities turned their attention more and more towards the land which they now wanted to take control by any means for their financial, political, economic and social security.[8]

In this background, after the Battle of Plassey in 1757, when the last independent ruler of Mughal Bengal was displaced by conspiracy and the Battle of Buxar, 1765 overthrew Mir Qasim, the fate of Bengal was sealed. In Bengal was started the Dual system of Government, where the English East India Co. had no responsibility but to enjoy the fruits of revenue collection while the Nawab of Bengal had all the responsibility from collecting revenue to conducting Faujdari or criminal cases and submitting the collected revenue to the government treasury and hence had no opportunity to enjoy the fruits of revenue collection.[9]

So gradually the English East India Co. transformed itself from a mere trading company to an administrative ruler. With this also began land revenue reforms which changed the landlord- subject relationship. Also a striking change gradually occurred in the social fabric of India. It is to be noted that due to the land revenue reforms like Permanent Settlement (1793), The Ryotwari and the Mahalwari Systems the relationship between the landlords and the ryots or peasantry was redefined especially in the case of Permanent Settlement. As regards the Permanent Settlement, which was mainly effected in Bengal, while the other two were

[8] Sekhar Bandopadhyay-From Plassey To Partition, p. 73.
[9] R.C. Majumdar (ed.)-Advanced History of India.

made effective in North India and South India respectively, due to defaultment in paying land revenue, which was due to be paid by the last day of the Bengali New Year, many old zamindars from the Mughal period were replaced by new town based moneyed classes who were mainly Hindus. On the other hand the composition of the subjects remained the same *i.e.* mostly Muslims. So there was every prospect that the communal fabric which remained intact even in the days of the Muslim rule was likely to be disturbed.[10]

Looking back on the social side some transformations were taking shape replacing the old traditionality and superstitions which were the main basis of the orthodox Hindu society. The introduction of vernacular education and western education in order to create an intermediate class between the English and the local subjects as well as some drastic social measures like abolition of sati, child marriage and introduction of widow rematriage affected the traditionality and orthodoxy of the old Hindu society. These changes affected the age old Hindu system and led to the creation of a class mainly Hindu Bengalees which acted as a bridge between the Hindus and English. As a result of this the Hindus accepted the educational changes and surged ahead than the others and moved closer to the English. This created a social gap between the Hindus and their Muslim counterparts.[11] In this context, the position of the Muslims *vis-a-vis* the Hindus have to be understood. Six centuries of Muslim rule had created a sense of complacency and superiority complex among them so much so when the English introduced western education in the 18th century, the Muslims were averse to taking up the opportunity. This was mainly due to their pride that they had been in the ruler's seats for six decades and taking up something from a community who were inferior or 'Kafer' was something which was against Islam and not approved by the Quran. And from this point they began to lag behind the Hindus. The Hindus who had no such rigidity were quick to take up the opportunity and developed

---

[10] Ibid.

[11] Tazeen M. Murshid-The Sacred and The Secular-Introduction.

closeness to the British. This backwardness of the Muslims led to the rise of antagonism *vis-a-vis* the Hindus.[12] Further, this aloofness of the Muslims from the British and their aversion to taking up modern educational programs of the time due to their prestige forced the British to blame the Muslims for the 1857 revolt. The rise of Sir Syed Ahmed Khan and his Aligarh Movement of 1878 was to be seen in this perspective. His constant persuasion of the British for some favours to the Muslim community due to their backwardness in contrast to the Hindus and his constant effort to convince the British of the loyalty of the Muslims to the British and that the Muslims were not responsible for the 1857 revolt ultimately bore fruits. But for this the Hindus were also no less responsible.

The introduction of vernacular and western education and the development of educational institutions now made the Hindus to think with reason and began to formulate an idea of forming an organization which would put forward the voices of the masses to the British. Ironically, the British also thought of the same line as Allan Octavian Hume was trying to find some sort of mechanism through which the steam of grievances would gush out and would act as a safety valve for the British. It is to be mentioned here that the English were already plagued with Ilbert Bill controversy of 1878 and the peasant protests against the high rents and oppression of the zamindars. Thus was formed the Indian National Congress under the president ship of W. C. Bonnerjea at Bombay in 1885.[13]

Meanwhile, post 1857 another development took place. The transformation of the Hindu Bengalees from a politically ignorant class to a politically conscious community had made the alarm bells ringing for the British. They now changed their attitude towards the Muslims and began to make friendly overtures to them. They now realized the harshness of the situation and what was beginning to come. They now formulated a policy of divide and rule in order to keep the Hindus and Muslims always at

[12] Ibid.

[13] Sekhar Bandopadhyay-From Plassey To Partition; Introduction.

loggerheads. Also, they were convinced that Bengal was the nerve centre of politics and if Bengal could be divided then it would be more convenient for them to govern. So on the pretext of administrative efficiency Bengal was to be divided on 19th July, 1905[14]. Its main architect was the then Viceroy of India, Lord Curzon and his secretary of state H.H. Risley and Andrew Fraser. It is to be noted that in 1858 on the basis of Queen Victoria's proclamation the rule of English East India Co. was transferred to the London Government and India now became a colony of the British Crown and Governor General now changed into Viceroy.[15] In fact, this act of partitioning the province of Bengal has been tried before even during the time of Lord William Bentinck due to the vastness of the province, but no body acted upon it.[16] However, the overwhelming protests by the Hindus, against the partition of Bengal, and the fear in its wake, of reforms favouring the Hindus, now led the Muslim elite in 1906 to meet the Viceroy Lord Minto, and to ask for separate electorates for the Muslims.[17]

In conjunction, they demanded separate legislative representation reflecting both their status as former rulers and their record of cooperating with the British. This led in December 1906, to the founding of All India Muslim League in Dacca under the leadership of Nawab Salimullah Khan of Dacca and its cofounders were Md. Ali Jinnah and Abul Kasem Fazlul Huq. Although by this time Lord Curzon had resigned due to differences with his military chief Lord Kitchener and returned to England, the League favored his partition plan.[18]

The Muslim elites' position, which was reflected in the League's position, had crystallized gradually over the next three decades, beginning with the 1871 census of British India which had first estimated the population in Muslim majority region.[19] In fact in the three decades since that census the Muslim leaders had been

[14] Sekhar Bandopadhyay-From Plassey to Partition.
[15] Ibid.
[16] Percival Spear, p. 176.
[17] Sekhar Bandopadhyay-From Plassey to Partition.
[18] Ludden, p. 200.
[19] Sekhar Bandopadhyay-From Plassey to Partition.

facing public animosity from some of the new Hindu social and political groups like the Arya Samaj not only supported cow protection societies in their agitation, but also being frustrated at the 1871 census's Muslim numbers-organised reconversion events for the purpose of welcoming Muslims back to the Hindu fold. In the United Provinces, Muslims became anxious when in the late nineteenth century, political representation increased, giving more power to the Hindus and Hindus were politically mobilized in the Hindi-Urdu controversy and the anti-cow killing riots of 1893.[20]

In 1905, when Tilak and Lajpat Rai attempted to rise to leadership position in the Congress and the Congress itself rallied around symbolism of Kali, Muslim fears increased. It was not lost for many Muslims, for example, that the rallying cry of Bande Mataram had first appeared in the novel Anandamath where the Hindus fought against the Muslim oppressors.[21] Lastly, the Muslim elite like the Nawab of Dacca, Khwaja Salimullah Khan, who hosted the League's first meeting in his mansion at Shahbag was aware that a new province would be beneficial to the Muslims having political aspirations.[22] The 1916 Lucknow session of the Congress saw an unanticipated mutual effort by the Congress and the Muslim League to get united as in Turkey made alliance with Germany as also because the Caliphate got threatened to be dislodged by the British government. Since the Turkish Sultan or Khalifa had also sporadically claimed guardianship of the Holy sites of Mecca, Medina and Jerusalem, and since the British and the allies were now in conflict with Turkey, some Indian Muslims began to doubt about the religious neutrality of the British.

In the Lucknow Pact, the League joined the Congress in the proposal for greater self government that was campaigned for by Tilak and his supporters; in return the Congress accepted separate electorates for the Muslims in the provincial legislatures as well as the Imperial legislative council. In 1916 the Muslim League did

[20] Ibid.
[21] Ludden, p. 201.
[22] Ayesha Jalal, Jinnah - The Sole Spokesman.

not have a large following hardly between 500 and 800 members. In the League itself the Pact did not have unanimous backing as it was mainly negotiated by young party Muslim members from the United Provinces like the two Ali brothers Mohammad Ali and Shaukat Ali, who had embraced the Pan Islamic cause; however, it had the support of a young lawyer from Bombay Mohammad Ali Jinnah, who rose to leadership of both the Muslim League and Indian independence movement.[23] In December 1919, the Government of India Act 1919 or the Montague-Chelmsford Reforms were passed after much deliberation. The new Act enlarged the provincial and Imperial legislative councils and repealed the Government of India's recourse to the official majority in unfavorable votes. The communal representation which was an integral part of the Morley-Minto Reforms and more recently of the Congress-Muslim League-Lucknow Pact was reaffirmed with seats being reserved for the Muslims, Sikhs, Indian Christians, Anglo-Indians and domiciled Europeans in both provincial and Imperial Legislative Councils. These reservation of seats provided an opportunity for the Muslims to demand for a separate state for the Muslims on the basis of two nation theory in the days to come. This theory was an ideology that the primary identity and an unifying denomination of the Muslims in the subcontinent was their religion and therefore Indian Hindus and Muslims were two distinct nations regardless of other commonalities.[24] In fact the two nation theory was a founding principle of the Pakistan movement, the ideology of Pakistan as a Muslim nation state in South Asia and the Partition of India in 1947. The ideology that religion was the determining factor in defining the nationality of the Indian Muslims was undertaken by Mohammed Ali Jinnah who termed it as an awakening for the Muslims in the creation of the State of Pakistan. However people like Vinayak Damodar Savarkar first propagated it. It is generally believed that the movement for Muslim self awakening and identity was started by Ahmed Sirhindi (1564–1624), who fought against Emperor Akbar's religious syncretism Din-I-ilahi movement and was particularly intensified

[23] Ibid.

[24] Sekhar Bandopadhyay-From Plassey to Partition.

under the Muslim reformer Shah Waliullah (1703–1762), who because he wanted to give back the Muslims their self consciousness during the decline of the Mughal empire and the rise of non Muslim powers like the Marathas, the Jats and Sikhs launched a mass movement of religious education which made them conscious of their distinct nationhood which in turn culminated culminated in the form of Two Nation Theory[25] Historian Akbar Ahmed considered also Haji Shariatullah (1782–1840) and Syed Ahmad Barelvi (1786–1831) to be the forerunners of the Pakistan movement, because of their purist and militant reformist movements targeting the Muslims saying that reformers like Waliullah Barelvi and Shariatullsh were not demanding a Pakistan in the modern sense of nationhood. They were, however, instrumental in creating an awareness for the crisis looming for the Muslims and the need to create their own political organization. What Sir Sayyid did was to provide a modern idiom in which to Express the quest for Islamic identity. So many described thought that Sir Sayyed Ahmed Khan (1817–1898) as the architect of the Two Nation Theory. Sir Sayyed in January, 1883 speech in Patna talked of two different nations.[26]

In 1888, in a critical assessment of Indian National Congress, he also considered Muslims to be a nationality among many others.[27] He wrote, "The aims and objects of the Indian National Congress are based upon an ignorance of history and present day politics, they do not take into consideration that India is inhabited by different nationalities; they presuppose that the Muslims, the Marathas, the Brahmins, the Kshatriyas, the Banias, the Sudras, the Sikhs, the Bengalees, the Madrasis and the Peshwaris can all be treated alike and all of them belong to' the same nation. The Congress think's they can profess the same religion, that they speak the same language, that their way of life and customs are

[25] Ian Talbot-Pakistan's Emergence in Alain M Low, Robin W Winks (Eds.)-The Oxford History of The British Empire, Oxford University Press, pp. 253-264.

[26] M. Ikram Chagatai (ed.)-Shah Waliullah (1703–1762): His Religious and Political Thought, Sang-e-Meel Publication (2005), p. 275.

[27] Sekhar Bandopadhyay-From Plassey to Partition

the same[28] ...I consider the experiment which the Indian National Congress wants to make fraught with danger and suffering for all the nationalities of India especially for the Muslims.[29] More substantially and influentially, the poet-philosopher Muhammad Iqbal and Barrister Muhammad Ali Jinnah (1871–1948) translated the Two Nation Theory into the political reality of a nation-state.[30] Earlier the scholar Al Biruni (973–1048) observed at the beginning of the eleventh century that Hindus and Muslims differed in all matters and habits.[31] On March 23, 1940 at the Labore session of the Muslim League, Jinnah made a speech very similar to Al Biruni. Jinnah stated that the Hindus and Muslims belonged to two different philosophies, with different social customs and literature, with no intermarriage and based on conflicting ideas and concepts. Their outlook on life and of life was different and despite thousand years of history, the relations between the Hindus and Muslims could not attend the level of cordiality.[32]

The All India Muslim League, in attempting to represent Indian Muslims of the subcontinent were a distinct and separate nation from the Hindus. At first they demanded separate electorates, but when they came to the conclusion that the Muslims would not be safe in a Hindu dominated India, they began to demand a separate state. The League demanded self determination for Muslim majority areas in the form of a sovereign state promising minorities equal rights and safeguards in these Muslim majority areas.[33] In his book, Pakistan or The Partition of India, Bhimrao Ramji Ambedkar wrote "If Muslims truly and deeply desire Pakistan, their choice ought to be accepted for the interest and safety of India... The real explanation of the failure of the Hindu Muslim unity lies in the failure to realize that what stands between the Hindus and Muslims is not a mere matter of difference and

---

[28] Ram Ch. Guha-Makers of Mod. India, Harvard University Press, 2011, p. 65.

[29] Gerald James Larson-India's Agony Over Religion, Sunny Press, 1995, p. 184.

[30] Stanley Wolpert-Jinnah of Pakistan, Oxford University Press, pp. 47-48.

[31] Ibid.

[32] Ibid.

[33] Bhimrao Ramji Ambedkar-Pakistan or Partition of India, Thacker Limited (1945), p. 324.

this antagonism is not to be attributed to material causes. It is formed by causes which take their origin to the historical, religious, cultural and social antipathy, of which political antipathy is only a reflection. These form one deep river of discontent which being regularly fed by these sources keeps on mounting to a head and overflowing its ordinary channels. Any current of water flowing from another source, however, pure when joins it instead of alternating the colour or diluting its strength becomes lost in the main stream. The silt of this antagonism which this current has deposited has become permanent and deep. So long as this silt keeps on accumulating and so long as this antagonism lasts, it is unnatural to expect this antipathy to give place to unity.[33]

Muhammad Iqbal's statement explaining the attitude of Muslim delegates to the London Round Table Conference in December 1933, was a rejoinder to Nehru's statement. Nehru had said that the attitude of the Muslim delegation was based on reactionarism. Iqbal concluded with his rejoinder:

"This position can admit of only two alternatives. Either the Indian majority community will have to accept for itself the permanent position of an agent of British imperialism in the east or the country has to be redistributed on the basis of religious, historical and cultural affinities so as to do away with the question of and the electorates and the communal problem in its present form.[34]

Muhammed Ali Jinnah in his Presidential Address at the All India Muslim League session at Lahore on 23nd March. 1940, he explained:

It is extremely difficult to appreciate why Hindu friends fail to understand the real nature of Islam and Hinduism. They are not religions in the strict sense of the word, but are in fact, different and distinct social orders, and it is a dream that the Hindus and Muslims can ever evolve a common nationality, and this misconception of one Indian nation has troubles and will lead India

[34] Iqbal and the Pakistan Movement, Lahore, Iqbal Academy.

to destruction if we fail to revise our notion in time. The Hindus and Muslims belong to two different religious philosophies, social customs and literature. They neither intermarry nor intertwine together and indeed, they belong to two different civilizations which are based mainly on conflicting ideas and conceptions. Their aspect on life and life are different. It is quite clear that Hindus and Mussalmans derive their inspiration from different sources of history. They have different epics, different heroes and different episodes. Very often the hero of one is a foe of the other, and likewise their victories and defeats overlap. To yoke together two such nations under a single state, one is a numerical minority and the other as a majority, must lead to growing discontent and final destruction of any fabric that may be so built for the government of such a state.[35]

In 1944, Jinnah said: "We maintain and hold that Muslims and Hindus are two major nations by any definition or test of a nation. We are a nation of hundred million and what more we are a nation with our own distinctive culture and civilization, language and literature, art and architecture, names and nomenclature, sense of values and proportions, legal laws and moral codes, customs and calendar, history and tradition, and aptitude and ambitions. In short we have our own outlook on life and of life."[36] On the other hand, though Savarkar was a proponent of two nation theory, he never expressed the idea of dividing the nation. He was in proponent to create two different states for Muslims and Hindus.

In this background, although Choudhury Rahmat Ali produced a pamphlet in 1933, Now or Never, in which term, Pakistan, land of the pure, comprising the Punjab, North Western Frontier Province, Kashmir, Sindh, Balochistan was coined for the first time, the pamphlet did not attract political attention. A little later a Muslim delegation to the Parliamentary Committee on Indian Constitutional Reforms gave short shrift to the idea of Pakistan, calling it chimerical and impractical. In 1932, the British Prime

[35] Official website, Nazaria-e-Pakistan Foundation (Excerpts from the Presidential Address delivered by Muhammed Ali Jinnah in Lahore on March 22, 1940.

[36] Talbot and Singh, p. 31.

Minister Ramsay MacDonald accepted Ambedkar's demand seat reservation for the Depressed Classes in the Central and Provincial Legislatures. The Muslim League favored the award as it had the potential to weaken the caste Hindu leadership. However, Mahatma Gandhi, who was seen as a leading advocate for Dalit rights, went on a fast into death to persuade the British to repeal the award. Ambedkar had to back down when he saw Gandhi's life was threatened.[37]

Two years later, the Government of India Act, 1935 introduced provincial autonomy, increasing the number of voters in India to 35 million.[38] More significantly law and order issues were devolved for the first time from the British authority to provincial governments headed by the Indians.[39] This increased Muslim anxiety about eventual Hindu domination. In the 1937 provincial elections the Muslim League got majority in the Muslim minority regions such as the United Provinces, where it won 29 of the 64 seats reserved for the Muslims.[40] However, in the Muslim majority regions like the Bengal and the Punjab the regional parties outperformed the League.[41] In the Punjab, the Unionist Party of Sikander Hayat Khan, won the elections and formed a government with the support of Indian National Congress and the Shiromoni Akali Dal, which lasted five years.[42] In Bengal, the League had to share power with Abu Kasem Fazlul Huq's Krishak Praja Party. Incidentally, Huq's Krishak Praja Party, which got the majority in Bengal and who after being refused by the Congress over disagreement on prisoner release and abolition of rent, had to form a government with the support of the League.[43]

The Congress, on the other hand, with 716 wins out of 1585 provincial assembly seats, was able to form governments in 7 out of 11 provinces of British India. In its manifesto the Congress

[37] 'The Turning Point in 1932: On Dalit Representation', The Hindu, 3rd May, 2018.
[38] Talbot and Singh, p. 32.
[39] Ibid.
[40] Talbot and Singh, p. 32.
[41] Ibid.
[42] Ibid.
[43] Joya Chatterjee-Bengal Divided.

maintained that religious issues were of less importance than economic and social issues of the masses. However, the election revealed that the Congress had contested just 58 out of the total 482 Muslim seats, and out of these it had won only 26.[44] In UP, where the Congress won, it offered to share power with the League on condition that the League stop functioning as a representative only of Muslims, which the League refused.[45] This proved to be a mistake as it alienated the Congress further from the Muslim masses. In addition, the new UP provincial administration promulgated cow protection and the use of Hindi.[46] The Muslim elite in UP was further alienated, when they saw chaotic scenes of the new Congress Raj, in which the rural people who sometimes turned up in large numbers in Government buildings, were indistinguishable from the administrators and the law enforcement personnel.[47] The Muslim conducted it's own investigation into the conditions of Muslims under Congress governed provinces.[48] The findings of such investigations increased fear among the Muslim masses of future Hindu domination. The view that Muslims would be unfairly treated in an independent India dominated by the Congress was now a part of the public discourse of the Muslims.[49] With the outbreak of second world war in 1939, the Viceroy Lord Linlithgow declared war on India's behalf without consulting the Indian leaders, which led to the resignation of the Congress provincial ministry in protest. The Muslim League which functioned under state patronage, in contrast organized "Deliverance Day", celebrations and supported Britain in the war effort. When Linlithgow met with nationalist leaders, he gave the same status to Jinnah as was accorded to Gandhi, and a month later described the Congress as a "Hindu organization."[50]

---

[44] Talbot and Singh, p. 32.
[45] Ibid.
[46] Ibid.
[47] Ibid, pp. 32-33.
[48] Ibid, p. 33.
[49] Talbot and Singh, p. 33.
[50] Ibid, p. 34.

In March, 1940, in the League's three day annual session in Lahore, Jinnah gave a two hour speech in English. On the last day of the session, Jinnah made the Bengal Premier Abul Kasem Fazlul Huq to read and propose the Lahore Resolution, also known as the Pakistan Resolution, which was duly passed. After the passing of the Resolution, Jinnah commented Bengal Tiger was caged (Fazlul Huq, who was also known as Sher-e-Bangla or Bengal Tiger). It is to be noted that Fazlul Huq was for United Bengal within United India. So when the Pakistan Resolution was passed he protested but to no avail.[51] The Pakistan Resolution demanded the areas in which the Muslims are numerically in majority as in the North Western and East Zones of India should be grouped to constitute independent states in which the constituent units will be autonomous and sovereign. Thus, the dice was cast. The distrust for each other and the non compromising attitude of the leaders coupled with the precarious position of the British due to the second world war led to the partition of India though the mindset for it was there quite long ago especially among the Muslims. The final nail in the coffin was put on 16th August, 1946, the day of Hartal as called by the Muslim League for partitioning India. That day history witnessed blood bath which was unparalleled in world history, also known as the Great Calcutta Killing.[52] This incident had put to rest all the doubts of the future of India whose effect was felt even post partition.

[51] Amalendu Dey-Pakistan Prastab O Fazlul Huq (Bengali)
[52] Ibid.

3

HARI SINGH, NEHRU AND KASHMIR

The cleavage that has appeared in the Hindu Muslim relationship could not be mended. The stances of the two parties, the Congress and the Muslim League, who were speaking for their respective communities were clear and there could be no turning back from it. Moreover, the London government already with their backs to the wall due to a series of agitations starting from the Quit India Movement of 1942 to Indian Naval Muttiny of 1946, which showed the British the writings on the wall, coupled with the damage suffered by Great Britain due to the second world war, it was becoming difficult for them to maintain the colony of India.

Moreover, despite the provincial elections under the Govt. Of India Act, 1935, the Cripps Mission, and the Cabinet Mission etc. the two parties stuck to their decision of partitioning the subcontinent. The British government also had a desire to hand over the administration to the Indians as early as possible. For this Lord Mt. Batten was sent to India with a clear instruction to transfer power by no later than August, 1948. Accordingly Mt. Batten prepared a blue print for partitioning India, known as the Mt.Batten Plan and ultimately, India was partitioned in 1947.

The birth pangs of an independent India, however, resulted in another plight for the Indians *i.e.* the beginning of the Kashmir problem which continues to ail the subcontinent to this day. Let us have a look at the short history of Kashmir along with its demographic features as well the positions of Raja Hari Singh and Nehru which play major role in the Kashmir complexities till this day.

Jammu and Kashmir, was from 1846 until 1952, a princely state under the British empire in India and ruled by a Jamwal Rajout Dogra Dynasty. The Dogra State was founded by Dhruva Dev of Jamuwal Dynasty in the declining days of the Mughal empire in the 18th century.[1] The state was created in 1846 from the territories previously under Sikh empire after the first Anglo-Sikh War. The English East India Co. had annexed the Kashmir Valley, Jammu, Ladakh and Gilgit-Baltistan from the Sikhs, and then transferred it to Raja Gulab Singh of Jammu in return for an indemnity payment of Rs. 75,00,000 Nanakshahee Rupees. The Jammu state then asserted its supremacy among the Dugar states to the South of the Kashmir Valley. It's ascent reached its peak under Dhruva Dev's successor Raja Ranjit Dev (1728–1780), who was widely respected among the hill states.[2]

Towards the end of Ranjit Dev's rule, the Sikh Misls gained ascendancy and Jammu began to be contested by the Bhangi, Kanhaiya and Sukerchakia Misls. Around 1770, the Bgangi Misl attacked Jammu and forced Ranjit Dev to become a tributary. Brij Lal Dev, his successor was defeated by the Sukerchakia Misl under Mahan Singh, who sacked Jammu and plundered it. Thus Jammu lost its supremacy over the surrounding country.[3]

In 1808, Jammu itself was annexed to the Sikh empire by Maharaja Ranjit Singh, the son of Mahan Singh.[4] Gulab Singh, Dhruva Dev's direct descendant, was 16 years old when Jamnu was annexed to the Sikh empire. Gulab Singh and his two brothers Dhyan Singh and Suchet Singh went on to enrol with the Sikh forces. Gulab Singh soon distinguished himself in battle, and was

---

[1] Ashoka Jerat-Dogra Legends of Art and Culture, p. 22.
[2] Ibid. Also, K. M. Panikkar-Gulab Singh, 1930, p. 10.
[3] Ibid, pp. 10–12.
[4] Ibid.

awarded a jagir near Jammu. He was also allowed to keep an independent force. After the conquest of Kishtwar (1821) and the subjugation of Rajouri, he was made a hereditary Raja of Jammu in 1822, with an annual allowance of 300, 000 rupees. Ranjit Singh personally installed him as the Raja of Jammu. His brother Dhyan Singh received Poonch and Suchet Singh Ramnagar. Thus, the state of Jammu was reestablished after a gap of twenty years under the sovereignty of the Sikh empire. Gulab Singh proceeded to regain its preeminence among the hill states.[5]

By 1827, Gulab Singh brought under his control all the principalities lying between Kashmir and Jammu.[6] Dhyan Singh became the Lord Chamberlain and later, Prime Minister for Ranjit Singh. Gulab Singh acquired fame in the Sikh court as a warrior and an able manager of all states's affairs.[7]

After the first Anglo-Sikh War (1945–46), following an agreement with the British, the British transferred the territories between the Beas and the Indus including Kashmir valley and Hazara under the Treaty of Amritsar to Gulab Singh in return for a payment of 7.5 million rupees (half the indemnity demanded from the Sikhs). The British as well as the Sikh empire then recognized him as an independent Maharaja.[8] Gulab Singh entered Srinagar on November 9, 1846 as the Maharaja of Jammu and Kashmir.[9] The state of Jammu and Kashmir comprised disparate regions, religion and ethnicity. As per the British census of India, 1941, Jammu and Kashmir registered a Muslim majority population of 77%, a Hindu population of 20%, and a sparse population of Buddhists and Sikhs comprising the remaining 3%.[10]

The 1941 census reported that most of the Muslims in the Jammu province and its Jagirs were closely connected with the tribes of the Punjab and were of the same original stock as the

[5] Ibid, pp. 14–34.
[6] K. M. Panikkar, p. 37.
[7] Ibid, p. 47.
[8] Satinder Singh-Raja Gulab Singh's Role, 1971, pp. 52–53.
[9] K. M. Panikkar-Gulab Singh, 1930, pp. 118–119.
[10] Bose-Roots of Conflict, Paths To Peace, 2003, pp. 15–17.

Hindu elements of Jammu population; with the Gujjars being an important element. Among Jammu province's population the ethnic make up was composed of Arains, Jats, Sudhans, Gujjars and Rajputs etc.[11]

The Muslims living in the southern part of the Kashmir province (Baramullah and Anantnag districts) were of the same category as the Kashmiri Pandit community and were designated as Kashmiri Muslims. The population of Muzaffarabad District was partly Kashmiri Muslim, partly Gujjar and the rest belonged to the tribes of the neighbouring Punjab and North Western Frontier Province. The 1921 census report stated that the Kashmiri Muslims were sub divided into numerous sub castes such as at, Dar, Wain etc.[12]

The 1921 Census Report stated that Kashmiri Muslims formed 31% of the Muslim population of the entire princely state of Jammu and Kashmir.[13] The Muslims in the Kashmir valley are predominantly Sunni, like the Jammu's Muslims. However, nearly all Muslims in Ladakh are Shia.[14]

With this demographic background, Maharaja Hari Singh ascended the throne of Kashmir in 1925. Born on September 23, 1895 in Jammu, Singh was the son of Raja Amar Singh Jamwal, whose brother Pratap Singh was the king of the state. When Hari Singh's father died in 1909, the British took keen interest in his studies. After his basic education in Mayo College in Ajmer, Rajasthan, Singh went to the British run Imperial Cadet Corps in Dehradun for military training.[15]

At the age of 30, Singh ascended the throne of Jammu and Kashmir when his uncle Pratap Singh passed away in 1925. The arrival of Hari Singh marked a major change in the Dogra Dynasty.

[11] An ant Ram, Hira Nand Raina-Census of India, 1931, Vol. XXIV, Jammu and Kashmir State, Part I, Report.

[12] C. K. Mohamed-Census of India, Vol. XXII, Part I, 1921, Report.

[13] C. K. Mohamed-Census of India, 1921, Vol. XXII, Kashmir, Part I, Report.

[14] Christopher Snedden-Understanding Kashmir and Kashmiris, Oxford University Press, p. 7.

[15] Ibid.

According to Dr. M. Y. Ganie, a professor of history and director of Srinagar based Institute of Kashmir studies, after Hari Singh ascended the throne he took many measures. The Muslim population of the state was disenfranchised till his arrival. Hari Singh introduced rules under which children were forced to take up modern education in what came to be known as Jabri schools (Jabri means force).[16]

Hari Singh also wanted to restructure the state bureaucracy to improve governance. For this he started to import bureaucrats from other parts of British India especially from Bengal. However, Kashmiri Pandits who were more educated and had a better representation than their Muslim counterparts, resisted the move.[17]

According to Prof. Ganie, "The Kashmiri pandits under the Dogra regime were highly educated and intellectually very strong. They knew that importing officials from Bengal would have long term ramifications, on governance and policy, hence they resisted.[18] "They compelled the Maharaja to introduce State Subjects Law, which defined citizenship of of Jammu and Kashmir. (This might be the basis of the special status of Jammu and Kashmir). The tussle within the services became the foundation for the movement to protect the state's indigenous identity.[19]

A popular uprising against Hari Singh began in 1931, when Abdul Qadeer of SWAT (Modern day Pakistan), an employee of an English army officer, was put on trial for treason and conspiracy to overthrow the regime. Records suggested that 24 Kashmiris were killed that summer. The uprising against Hari Singh had begun and till date July 13, is remembered as Martyr's day across the valley.[20] Though Hari Singh largely contained the rebellions

---

[16] www.theprint.com-Article by Azan Javaid-Hari Singh, The Last Dogra King, who gave Jammu and Kashmir its special status.

[17] Ibid.

[18] Ibid.

[19] Article by Azaan Javaid-Hari Singh, the last Dogra King who gave Jammu and Kashmir its special status in www.theprint.com

[20] Ibid.

between 1931 and 1947, his real test came with the partition of British India. Hari Singh backed by his administration, wanted Jammu and Kashmir to remain as an independent region, espoused by his Prime Minister Ram Chandra Kak. But according to Two Nation Theory the state was supposed to join Pakistan on account of it being a princely state with Muslim majority.

Hari Singh even signed a Stand Still Agreement with Pakistan in order to maintain status quo till a final decision on Kashmir was agreed upon. India did not sign the Agreement. In the meantime, people from Chenab valley's Poonch region, in June 1947, raised arms against Hari Singh's Dogra soldiers even as the subcommittee was engulfed with communal riots.

The rebellion was carried out mostly by former Muslim soldiers of the British army who had returned from the first world war. The rebellion in Poonch of Jammu and Kashmir, was brutally suppressed by Singh's army which gave a newly created Pakistan a pretence to send over tribal militias. For long, India maintained that the tribal militias were Pakistani troops. This intervention by Pakistan was known as "Kabail Raid" in local parlance.[21]

Hari Singh who till then had successfully manoeuvred between India and Pakistan to remain independent was caught in a dilemma. Under pressure from the Nehru government to allow Indian troops in Kashmir to defend the region and suppress the insurgency Poonch, Hari Singh signed the Instrument of Accession to join India reluctantly. But this had not been an easy task and this brings us the question of Nehru and Hari Singh regarding the latter's consent to accede to India.[22]

Dr. Sheikh Showkat Hussain, a Kashmir based political expert noted that this period of Hari Singh was marked by his transformation from a feudal ruler to a despot as it was under the eyes of Hari Singh that the "Jammu Massacre" or mass killing of Muslims in Jammu region during the partition took place.[23]

---

[21] Ibid.
[22] Ibid.
[23] Ibid. Also, Christopher Snedden-Kashmir: The Unwritten History.

Hussain further added, "Even though he reluctantly signed the temporary Instrument of Accession to India, he did not give consent for the application of the same for the future of Jammu and Kashmir. But despite that the brutal crackdown in Jammu region is a testimony to the fact that he had become a despot. However, he alone cannot be blamed for the Jammu Massacre. At the time Sheikh Abdullah was appointed as the Head of the emergency administration by the Maharaja. Also, here we have to look into the relationship between Nehru and Sheikh Abdullah in this context as Sheikh Abdullah was appointed the Prime Minister of Jammu and Kashmir.[24]

On 26th October, 1947, Raja Hari Singh signed the Instrument of Accession with Lord Mountbatten, the then Viceroy of India. Incidentally, Hari Singh had no friends in the Congress except Sardar Vallabh Bhai Patel, but the latter was helpless to protect Hari Singh as Mohandas Karamchand Gandhi did not like the Maharaja more due to the incident of Jammu Massacre, where many innocent Muslims were killed.[25]

At the time of partition of India in 1947, the British gave up their suzerainty over the princely states, which were left with the option of joining India or Pakistan or remaining independent. Maharaja Hari Singh indicated his preference to remain independent of the new dominions. All the major political groups of the state supported his decision, except for the Muslim Conference which declared in favour of accession to Pakistan on 19th July, 1947. (Eventually they agreed on a modified resolution which respectfully and fervently appealed to the Maharaja to declare internal autonomy of the State... and accede to the dominion of Pakistan. However, the General Council did not challenge the Maharaja's right to take a decision on accession, and it acknowledged that his rights should be protected even after acceding to Pakistan).[26] In fact, the Muslim Conference was popular in the Jammu province of the state. It was closely allied

[24] Ibid.

[25] An article by S. Sharma in www.quora.com.

[26] Balraj Puri-The Question of Accession, Epilogue, pp. 4–6.

with the All India Muslim League, which was set to inherit Pakistan.[27] Unlike the Kashmir valley which remained mostly calm during this transition period, the Jammu province which was contiguous to the Punjab, experienced mass migration that led to violent inter religious activity. Large numbers of Hindus and Sikhs from Rawalpindi and Sialkot started arriving since March, 1947, bringing "harrowing stories of Muslim atrocities in West Punjab." This provoked counter violence on Jammu Muslims almost like in Sialkot.[28] Ilyas Chattha writes, "The Kashmiri Muslims were to pay a heavy price in September-October, 1947 for the earlier violence in the West Punjab.[29]

According to scholar Ian Copland, the administration's against its Muslim subjects in Jammu was undertaken partly out of revenge for the Poonch rebellion that started earlier.[30] Observers stated that a main aim of Hari Singh and his administration was to alter the demographic position of the region by eliminating the Muslim population, in order to ensure Hindu majority in the region.[31]

Scholars like Ilyas Chattha, and Jammu journalist Ved Bhasin had blamed the mishandling of the law and order by Maharaja Hari Singh and his army in Jammu for the large scale communal violence in the region.[32] In fact, this communal upsurge was a common scene in Eastern India and Northern India which broke out as a result of partition and transfer of population. In eastern part of the country the most suffered region was Bengal and in the northern side the United Provinces and the Punjab sufferings from communal violence had no parallels in the annals of history.

On 14th October, 1947 the RSS activists and the Akalis attacked various villages of Jammu district like Amrey, Cheak, Atmapura,

27 Ibid.

28 A. G. Noorani-Horrors of Partition, Frontline, p. 39.

29 Chattha-Partition And Its Aftermath, 2009, p. 179.

30 Ian Copland-State, Community and Neighborhood in Princely North India, 1900–1950, Palgrave MacMillan, 2005, p. 143

31 Bed Bhasin-"Jammu, 1947"- Kashmir Life. Also, A. G. Noorani-Horrors of Partition, Frontline, p. 29.

32 Ibid.

Kochpura and after murdering the Muslims, looted their properties and set their houses on fire. Muslims were killed enmass in and around the city of Jammu. It was said the state troops led the attack and arms as well as ammunition were provided to the rioters by the state officials. It seemed to be preplanned as the Government had disabled a large number of Muslim soldiers in the state army and had discharged Muslim police officers.[33] According to the account of the refugees, the Maharaja was "in person commanding all the forces which were ethnically cleansing the Muslims.[34] Most of the Muslims outside the Muslim dominated areas were murdered by communal rioters moving in vehicles with fully loaded arms, though officially the city of Jammu was declared under curfew. It seemed that the curfew was imposed to restrict the movements of the Muslims.[35] Many Gujjar men and women who supplied milk to the city from the surrounding areas were found massacred enroute. It was said that Ramnagar reserve in Jammu was littered with dead bodies of Gujjar men, women and children. In the Muslim locality of Jammu city, like in Talab Khatikan and Mohalla Ustad, Muslims after being laid siege were denied food and water. They were eventually asked to surrender and leave for Pakistan for their safety and security. These Muslims and others who wanted to go to Sialkot in thousands were loaded in trucks and escorted by the troops. In the first week of November, when they reached the outskirts of the city, they were pulled out and killed by armed RSS men and Sikhs, while abducting the women.

Mahatma Gandhi commented on the situation in Jammu on 25th December, 1947, in his speech at a prayer meeting in New Delhi, "The Hindus and Sikhs of Jammu and those who had gone there from outside had killed the Muslims. The Maharaja of Kashmir was responsible for what is happening there....a large number of Muslims have been killed and Muslim women have been

[33] Chattha-Partition and Aftermath, 2009, p. 180, 182.

[34] Chattha-Partition And Its Aftermath, 2009, p. 180–182.

[35] Ved Bhasin-Jammu 1947, Kashmir Life. Ibid. Also, Khalid Bashir Ahmed-Circa 1947, "A Long Story", Kashmir Life.

dishonoured.[36] Bhasin said that the massacres took place in the presence if the then Jammu and Kashmir's Prime Minister Mehr Chand Mahajan, and the governor of Jammu, Lala Chet Ram Chopra.[37] To be noted that on 16th November, 1947 Skeikh Abdulah arrived in Jammu.[38]

Countering the above incidents, the Western districts of Poonch and Mirpur saw armed uprising by Pashtun tribes-men of North Western Frontier Province and the adjoining princely states and the tribal areas in the first week of October, 1947. The Hindus and the Sikhs were driven out from there to the towns where the state troops were garrisoned. From October 24, 1947, the rebels took total control of the towns Bhimber (24th October), Rajouri (7th November), Mirpur (25th November), and Deva Vatala. The Hindus and the Sikhs were totally annihilated.[39] In Rajouri according to sources over 30000 Hindus and Sikhs were massacred.[40] In Mirpur, over 20000 Hindus and Sikhs were dead or missing.[41]

Under these extremely critical circumstances, Maharaja Hari Singh's dream of keeping Kashmir independent of both India and Pakistan was shattered as the threat of Pakistan army loomed before him. Now he sent his deputy prime minister Ram Lal Batra with the proposal of accession and sent two letters in December, 1947-one to the then Indian Prime Minister Jawharlal Nehru and the other to Sardar Vallabh Bhai Patel were sent seeking military help. Even though Batra had reached Delhi, and Meher Chand, the Prime Minister of Jammu and Kashmir under Hari Singh was already there, little signs of Indian troops movement to Srinagar

---

36 "Document Twenty", The Second Assassination of Gandhi by Ram Puniyani, Anamika Pub. & Distributors, 2003, pp. 91–92.

37 Ved Bhasin-Jammu 1947, Kashmir Life.

38 Ibid. Also, Khalid Bashir Ahmed-Circa 1947, "A Long Story", Kashmir Life.

39 Dasgupta-Jammu and Kashmir, 2012, p. 97. According to Ananda Bazar Patrika, May, 2019, for protesting against the massacre Sheikh Abdullah was arrested on 20th May, 1946. At the request of Nehru to Hari Singh, he was released.

40 Sri Nandan Prasad, Sri Dharm Pal-Operations in Jammu and Kashmir, 1947–48. History Division, Ministry of Defense, Government of India, pp. 49–50.

41 Christopher Snedden-Kashmir the Unwritten History, 2013, p. 56. Also, Dasgupta-Jammu and Kashmir, 2012, p. 97 and Hassan-Mirpur, 1947, 2013.

could be noticed.[42] Mohammad Ali Jinnah, at that time the Prime Minister of Pakistan, meanwhile, wanted his British Commander in Chief, to send the Pakistani army officially and take over the state. However, the British military officer refused to follow this order and told Jinnah that he could not do it without consulting Supreme Commander of all forces remaining in India and Pakistan, Field Marshal Claude Auchinlake.[43] Before this, Meher Chand Mahajan who was made the Prime Minister of Jammu and Kashmir by Raja Hari Singh at the request of Sardar Vallabh Bhai Patel in May, 1947, had a meeting with Nehru on October 26, 1947, where he proposed to both Nehru and Patel: "Give army, take accession, and give whatever powers you want to give to the popular party (National Conference headed by Sheikh Abdullah), but the army must fly to Srinagar this evening, otherwise I will go and negotiate terms with Jinnah as the city must be saved. Nehru was obviously visibly upset at Mahajan's proposal of even contemplating the idea of talking to Jinnah and told him to leave the room. Even Patel whispered in his ears when he was walking out of the room, "Of course, you are not going to Pakistan."[44]

At the same time present in Nehru's residence was the popular Kashmiri mass leader and future chief minister of the state of Jammu and Kashmir, Sheikh Abdullah, who had overheard the entire exchange.[45]

"Sheikh Abdullah, who was staying in the Prime Ministers' house, was over hearing the talks. Sensing a critical moment, he sent in a slip of paper to the Prime Minister. The Prime Minister read it and said that both the Sheikh and Mahajan were of the same opinion.[46]

Abdullah was completely against the merger of the state with Pakistan since the then large Kashmiri population did not buy

---

[42] Article by Rinchen Norbu Wangchuk-Untold Story- How One Note To Nehru Changed The Fate of Jammu and Kashmir in www.thebetterindia.com.
[43] Ibid.
[44] Meher Chand Mahajan's Autobiography, Hindustan Times, 1947.
[45] Mahajan's Autobiography, The Hindustan Times, 1947.
[46] Ibid.

Jinnah's Two Nation Theory, which envisioned the creation of a new separate states of Jammu and Kashmir along religious lines.[47]

The following morning, the Indian armed forces made their way into Srinagar with Maharaja's offer of accession and promise of transferring of power to Sheikh Abdullah. Days after the Indian troops arrived at Srinagar, Sheikh Abdullah took the charge of the adhoc administration, and in the following months took over as the Prime Minister of the state.[48]

In other parts of the state meanwhile, the Indian armed forces aided by the locals had repulsed the tribals and sent them packing.[49]

So, finally on October 26, 1947, Maharaja Hari Singh signed the Instrument of accession to India. "Now, therefore, I, Shriman Inder Mahander Rajrajeswar Maharajadhiraj Shri Hari Singhji, Jammu and Kashmir Naresh Tatha Tibetadi Deshadhipathi, Ruler of Jammu and Kashmir, in the exercise of sovereignty in and over my said State do hereby execute this my Instrument of Accession." By signing on this legal document, on October 26, 1947, Maharaja Hari Singh agreed that the State would become a part of India. But it has not been an easy affair.[50]

Note: At the time Maharaja Hari Singh was pleading for help in the face of Pakistan's tribal invasion, Jinnah had decided to celebrate Eid at Srinagar. Meher Chand Mahajan in his Autobiography wrote that Jinnah ordered his British Commander in Chief to march two brigades of Pakistani army to Jammu and Kashmir on October 27, 1947, one from Rawalpindi and the other from Sialkot. The Sialkot Brigade was to capture Jammu and Kashmir as well as Hari Singh, while the Rawalpindi Brigade was to reach Srinagar, but the British officer refused to march his troops to fight those of another, which also belonged to U.K. without consulting the Supreme Commander of both the dominions. But

[47] Ibid.
[48] Ibid.
[49] Ibid.
[50] Mehr Chand's Autobiography in The Hindustan Times, 1947.

on October 26, 1947, the Supreme Commander Claude Auchinlake informed Jinnah that Jammu and Kashmir had acceded to the Indian dominion. The next morning, the Indian army landed at Srinagar.

The founder of Pakistan, Mohammed Ali Jinnah, had perhaps assumed that Kashmir, by the logic of its majority Muslim population, would become a part of his country. But a few years before partition, when he sent an aide to Kashmir for an assessment, the conclusion was sobering: "No important religious leader has ever made Kashmir... his home or even an ordinary centre of Islamic activities," the side reported. "It will require a considerable period of time to reform them and convert them to true Islam."[51]

Hari Singh, in the weeks after August 15, 1947 gave no indication of giving up his state's independence. Pakistan then decided to force the issue when on October 24, 1947, thousands of tribal Pathans swept into Kashmir.[52]

On 25th October, 1947 V. P. Menon considered to be close to Patel, flew to Srinagar to get Hari Singh's nod for Kashmir's accession to India. On October 26, 1947, Hari Singh and his Dunbar shifted to Jammu, to the safety of Maharaja's winter palace, and out of harm's way from the marauding tribes-men. And ultimately, on October 26, 1947, the accession to India was completed.[53]

On October 27, 1947, the Ist Sikh battalion flew into Srinagar. Srinagar was soon secured from the Pakistani invaders but the battles in the larger regions were just beginning. Despite Field Marshal Claude Auchinlake's refusal to send troops to Kashmir, Jinnah finally sent his military personnel to Kashmir but by then Indian forces had taken control of nearly two-thirds of the state. However, Gilgit and Baltistan territories were occupied by Pakistani forces. The fighting between the Indian troops and

---

[51] Article on Hari Singh's Signing of Instrument of Accession in www.mapsofindia.com
[52] Ibid.
[53] Ibid.

Pakistani tribesmen and forces continued for more than a year after accession, which was known as the first Indo-Pak War.[54] Finally, a United Nations ceasefire was arranged at the end of 1948. After long negotiations, the ceasefire was accepted by both the countries and was put into effect. The terms of the ceasefire laid out in the United Nations Resolution of August 13 1948 were adopted by the U.N. on January 5, 1949.[55]

It is true that tragedy is not found in the conflict between good and evil but between one good being and another, who were victims of circumstances and prisoner of their own character having all their flaws amidst qualities. Jawharlal Nehru and Sheikh Abdullah were committed secularists and close friends. Each overrode the distrust his colleagues tried to instill in his mind about the friend. They fell out and Nehru want only humiliated his friend, got him sacked as the Prime Minister of Jammu and Kashmir and put Sheikh Abdullah behind bars for eleven years, except for a few months' break in 1958.[56] Neither fully reflected the psyche of his people or his associates. Patel's letter of June 19, 1946 to another friend reflected Nehru's outlook on Kashmir ("a Hindu state situated in Muslim surrounding") and distrust of Sheikh Abdullah.[57]

To Nehru, Sheikh Abdullah was Kashmir. "For me the people of Kashmir were basically represented by you," Nehru wrote to his friend on April 25, 1952 as differences arose between them.[58] He had good reason to do so because Indira Gandhi wrote to him on May 14, 1948 "They say only Sheikh Abdullah is confident of winning the plebiscite" in Kashmir. On his return from his visit to the State, Vice President S. Radhakrishnan told President Rajendra Prasad that "even Sheikh Abdullah thought we would

[54] Article on Hari Singh's signing of the Instrument of Accession in www.mapsofindia.com.
[55] Ibid.
[56] Jammu and Kashmir: 1949–64: Select Correspondence Between Jawharlal Nehru and Karan Singh edited by Jamaid Alam, Penguin, p. 4.
[57] Ibid.
[58] Selected Works of Jawharlal Nehru; Volume 18, p. 388.

lose in a plebiscite." The President conveyed that to Nehru on July 14, 1953.[59]

Contrary to Nehru's claim, Sheikh Abdullah was by no means representative of Jammu and Kashmir. On the issue of accession, public opinion was divided. Indira Gandhi sensed that the majority favored Pakistan. Sheikh Abdullah favored India because of its secular ideals.[60] Ideally, he would have favored India-Pakistan accord in Kashmir that guaranteed the State's autonomy and ensured peace. Pakistan's tribal raid forced the pace.[60]

The Sheikh bared his outlook in a 'secret' talk with the United States ambassador Loy Henderson in Srinagar, which was reported to the State Department on September 29, 1950. Abdullah was "vigorous in restating that in his opinion it (Kashmir) should be independent; that overwhelming majority population desired this independence... Kashmir... people had language and cultural background of their own. Their Hindus customs and traditions widely differed from Hindus in India, and outlook and background; their Muslims also quite different from the Muslims of Pakistan. Fact was that population of Kashmir was homogeneous inspire of presence of Hindu minority. But independent Kashmir could exist only in case it had friendship with both India and Pakistan; in case both these countries had friendly relations with each other."[61]

Abdullah was opposed to the partition of Jammu and Kashmir. "If a choice had to be made, it would be preferable for Kashmir to go to India than to Pakistan. It would be disastrous for the Kashmiris to be brought under the control of government with medieval Koranic outlook."[62]

This was the thought of a secular Kashmiri nationalist. He preferred India because of its secular ideals. Once Nehru in a public rally at Calcutta on I[st] January, 1952, commented,"...At the moment

[59] Ibid.

[60] Jammu and Kashmir: 1949–64: Selected Correspondence between Jawharlal Nehru and Karan Singh, ed. by Jamaid Alam, Penguin, pp. 4–7.

[61] Ibid.

[62] Ibid.

it is Sheikh Abdullah who is completely opposed to Pakistan. There is no doubt about that he is the leader of the people of Kashmir, a very great leader. If tomorrow Sheikh Abdullah wanted Kashmir to join Pakistan, neither I nor all the forces of India would be able to stop it because if the leader decides it will happen."[63]

Nehru also knew that the Sheikh had, as he put it, waded through blood to shake hands with India. He once reminded Patel on December 30, 1947, "... Sheikh Abdullah had to keep the goodwill of the Muslims to some extent even in Jammu.[64]

Abdullah minced no words in telling Patel, the protector of Maharaja Hari Singh, on October 10, 1948, "I regret that inspite of my repeated attempts in this behalf the sentiments of the people of this State with regard to the unmistakable part which the Maharaja and his satellites took in the general massacre of Muslims in Jammu are but insufficiently appreciated." He quoted from a note of June 1, 1948, in which he recalled Hari Singh's flight from Srinagar to Jammu, as the raiders came in and the organized killings of Muslims in Jammu "for weeks under his very nose" a few miles from the palace. H had written about this to Nehru and Gandhi in December, 1947.[65]

Nehru pleaded with the Maharaja on December 1, 1947, to make amends. "If here is going to be plebiscite, then obviously we have to work in such a way as to gain the goodwill of the majority of the population of the State, which means chiefly the Muslims. The policy recently pursued in the Jammu province ha alienated the Muslims there very greatly and has created a great deal of Ill-feeling in certain parts of the country. The only person who can effectively deal with the situation is Sheikh Abdullah... Even if military forces held Kashmir for a while, the later consequence might be a strong reaction against this. Essentially, therefore, this is a problem of psychological approach to the mass of the people and of making them feel that they will be benefited by being within

[63] Ibid.
[64] S. P. C., Volume I, p. 143.
[65] S. P. C., Volume 1, pp. 134–137

the Union. If the average Muslim feels that he has no safe or secure place in the Union, then obviously he will look elsewhere.[66]

Spitting the state would not do. This was Hari Singh's proposal, Nehru warned Patel on April 17, 1949. "This idea is based on the belief that a plebiscite for the whole of Kashmir is bound to be lost and therefore let us save Jammu at least. You will perhaps remember that some proposal of this kind was put forward by the Maharaja some months back. It seems to me that this kind of propaganda is very harmful indeed for us. Whatever may happen in the future, I do not think Jammu province is running away from us. If we want Jammu province by itself and are prepared to make a present of the rest to Pakistan, I have no doubt I can clinch the issue in a few days. The prize we are finding for is the valley of Kashmir.[67]

By 1952, Nehru was in favour of reducing tha autonomy of Jammu and Kashmir. The Delhi Agreement between him and the Sheikh gave him the veto on the appointment of Sadr-I-riyasat even after his election by the State's legislature, his continuance of office depended on the Centre's whim.[68]

Nehru's relations with Abdullah deteriorated when he wrote his infamous note of August 25, 1952 calling Kashmiris "not what are called a virile people. They are soft and addicted to easy living." After a stunning confession that public pledges not withstanding, he had decided privately in 1948 not to hold a plebiscite and asked Sheikh Abdullah to get it ratified by the Constituent Assembly. But the Sheikh found it difficult to accept as the Kashmiris were already disenchanted with him and India.[69] On the other hand, Nehru was under tremendous pressure from his fellow colleagues especially Karan Singh who demanded complete accession of the state to India. Incidentally, under the Instrument of Accession Maharaja Hari Singh agreed for a partial

[66] Ibid.
[67] Ibid.
[68] Ibid.
[69] SWJN, Volume 19, pp. 322–323.

accession to India and Sheikh Abdullah requested for a special status for Jammu and Kashmir. Interestingly, the Sheikh agreed to accede to India on Nehru's promise of special status for Jammu and Kashmir. Karan Singh did not support the break to lineage of the Dogra dynasty as he himself belonged to it and proposed if complete accession was not possible then trifurcate the state into Ladakh, Kashmir Valley and Jammu. Strangely, Karan Singh also urged Nehru to go for referendum if plebiscite was not possible.[70]

Apparently facing pressure from Nehru, his own brethrens and the Hindu members of the Constituent Assembly, Sheikh Abdullah now reverted to his old theme that only India Pakistan accord can end the uncertainty and ensure peace and advocated it openly. His National Conference set up a committee to consider possible solutions and Nehru as well as Maulana Azad were informed of it. A special session of the National Conference was called at the Sheikh's residence in May, 1953. Three main issues which were discussed are the following: (A) The political situation *vis-a-vis* the India-Pakistan dispute over Kashmir (B) Application of fundamental rights to the people of Jammu and Kashmir, (C) Extension of the jurisdiction of the Supreme Court to Jammu and Kashmir state.[71]

The committee came to the conclusion that the internal stability of the State was impossible so long as international settlement on the final affiliation of the state was not achieved. An extract from the final settlement of the Committee's minute held in June 9, 1953, reads: As a result of the discussion held in the course of various meetings the following proposals only emerge as an alternative for an honourable and peaceful solution of the Kashmir dispute between India and Pakistan: (a) Overall plebiscite with conditions as detailed in the minutes of the meeting dated 4.6.1953 (b) Independence of the whole state and (c) Independence of the whole state with joint control (India-Pakistan) of foreign affairs

---

70 Ibid.

71 Frontline, Volume 25, Issue 25, December 16–29, article by A. G. Noorani- Kashmir, blunder from the past.

and defences. (d) The Dixon Plan for independence of the plebiscite area.[72]

In June,1953 Maulana Azad had visited Kashmir and was apprised of the proceedings. Early in July, 1953 Nehru was informed of the decision. He was shortly going to have a meeting with the Prime Minister of Pakistan Mohammedali Bogra, to discuss and find an early solution to the Kashmir dispute.[73]

Nehru in his talks, disappproved of the idea of independence, but apparently not of the deliberation themselves about the future of the state. He met Mohammedali Bogra from July 25 to July 27, 1953 to decide the future of the state. Early in August, 1953, Sheikh Abdullah had called a meeting of the Working Commitee of the General Council in the third and fourth weeks in order to review the situation. On August 8, 1953, just two days before the scheduled Cabinet Meeting, Sheikh Abdullah was arrested at the dead of night along with a number of his colleagues.[74]

Having tinkered with Article 370 of the Constitution, Nehru belatedly offered to make it permanent. But Abdulla's letter of July 16, 1953 to Azad recorded why he declined the offer.

"Even after the Delhi Agreement responsible spokesman of the government of India declared that their ultimate objective was to secure the complete merger of the State with India and that they waited for appropriate time and conditions to bring that about. These statements reveal that the Delhi Agreement could not provide a basis to finalize the relationship between India and Kashmir, but that it (Delhi Agreement) provided temporary arrangements to finalize accession. The only difference between the Government of India and various other elements in the country on the issue is whether to bring about the merger of the state with India now or after sometime.... I am very happy to hear from you

[72] Jammu and Kashmir: 1949–1964: Selected Correspondence Between Jawharlal Nehru and Karan Singh, Penguin, ed. By Jamaid Alam.

[73] Ibid.

[74] Sheikh Abdullah in his letter from jail to G. M. Sadiq dated September 26, 1956, published in Sheikh-Sadiq Correspondence August to October, 1956, p. 18.

that the Government of India is willing to declare that the special position given to Kashmir will be made permanent and that the Government of India would be bound by it without any condition. If such a declaration had been made at an appropriate time, it would undoubtedly have strengthened our hands and unified various organizations and public opinion in the state and even if the masses had been asked about accession, a majority of them would have come out in favor of India.[75] But unfortunately that was not to be.

The changes effected on various occasions in the relationship between India and Kashmir greatly agitated public opinion and also weakened our hands to a great extent. Although such a declaration is welcome it remains to be seen if it would draw the support of different sections of people in India and Kashmir. Sheikh Abdullah was prepared to parley but Nehru not. He had ruled out harleys with Pakistan on anything but Status Quo. The Sheikh knew there could be no solution without any India Pakistan accord.[76]

The Sheikh had begun to bow to Kashmiri opinion, not to Nehru. Even at the best of times he had made known his reservations on accession and asserted his independence. He said at Hazratbal on April 25, 1952, "It would be better to die than to submit to the taunt that India is our bread-giver." He explained to Nehru on May 2, 1952 that he had sought to counteract the propaganda "we were being kept in the saddle with the help of the Indian bayonets. He drew his power from the people, they from New Delhi. He had his hand on the pulse of the people, they on their master's pulse.[77]

---

[75] Ibid.

[76] Jammu and Kashmir: 1949–1964: Selected Correspondence between Jawharlal Nehru and Karan Singh: *ed.* by Jamaid Alam, Penguin. In fact, Sheikh Abdullah by the Delhi Agreement on the basis of promise of Art. 35A *i.e.* special status to Jammu and Kashmir gave consent to become Prime Minister of the state. Article 35A states that only the original residents of Jammu and Kashmir region would have the right to sell or buy property or any other accessibility.

[77] SWJN, Volume 18 pp. 387 & 390.

Sheikh Abdullah was battling against the tide of public opinion since the accession. Hence, the proposal he gave to the British Commonwealth Secretary Patrick Gordon-Walker in New Delhi, on February, 20 1948, in New Delhi, in the presence of Nehru, Sheikh Abdullah said that he thought that the solution was that Kashmir should accede to both the Dominions with its autonomy jointly guaranteed by them.[78] Nehru, however, was against plebiscite but in public wanted to stand by the side of the people. It is to be mentioned here that at the outbreak of I^st^ Indo-Pak War in 1947, the Government of India without any prior consultation nor informing the Parliament referred the Kashmir issue to the U.N.O. Security Council on 1st January, 1948, under Article 35 of the U.N. Charter.[79]

Following set up of the United Nations Commission for India and Pakistan (UNCIP), the U.N. Security Council passed Resolution 47, on 21st April, 1948. The U.N. asked both the parties to return to their previous position but Pakistan dilly dallied. Following the ceasefire of hostilities it also established U.N. Military Observer Group (UNMOGIP) to monitor the ceasefire.

Once normalcy was restored and the environment remained congenial then free and fair plebiscite would be held. Having referred the Kashmir issue to the U.N.O, Nehru because of his closeness to Sheikh Abdullah at that time was confident of winning the plebiscite in his favour. But after 1952 when differences arose between the Sheikh and Nehru over the status of Kashmir, this plebiscite was shelved. The government of Sheikh Abdullah was dismissed, the Legislative was dissolved in 1956 and Article 370 was granted. By this article Jammu and Kashmir was granted autonomy to govern with defences, foreign affairs and economy lying with the Centre. In 1957, Nehru once confessed to one of his close aides Balraj Puri that given the volatile situation in Kashmir, they had been playing with fire and question of plebiscite would wait. However, in 1964, India's non-permanent representative at

[78] Ibid.

[79] Karel Wellens-Resolutions and Statements of United Nations Security Council (1946–1988).

the U. N. Security Council, Mohammad Karim Chagla made it clear that due to situation in Kashmir not being conducive the question of plebiscite could not be considered in the near future.[80] From this time onwards every power be Pakistan or India have used Kashmir to serve their political interests.

[80] An Article in the Ananda Bazar Patrika, May, 2019.

4

INDO-PAK RELATIONS-A TIME LINE

India and Pakistan though share a common past have a tumultuous relationship between them since partition and their births as two separate independent dominions in 1947. Incidentally, Pakistan was born on 14th August, 1947 and India on 15th August, 1947 and since then India is having a tryst with her destiny. The Hindu Muslim animosity had made the relationship between the two communities to reach a point of no return. Hence, finally under the stewardship of the then Viceroy Lord Mountbatten and on the basis of India Independence Act, India was partitioned on 15th August, 1947. The day before *i.e.* on 14th August, 1947, Pakistan was born. Along with this was introduced a new era of relationship between India and Pakistan, which was bitter and marked by intermittent violence and blood shed, its central point being Kashmir. It is to be noted that before the partition Jinnah in his blueprint had already demanded Jammu and Kashmir be included within Pakistan. But when the draft plan was shown Jinnah's dreams remained unrealized. A series of communal violence starting with the Great Calcutta killing of 16th August, 1946 now opened the pandora box. So when India was partitioned and Kashmir acceded to India, Jinnah as an act of revenge in order to keep India on tenterhooks sent tribal invaders to Kashmir on 26th October, 1947, thus triggering on the Ist Indo-Pak War of 1947–48. It also caused one of the largest migrations that history has ever witnessed.

The first Indo-Pak War was fought after armed tribesmen (Lashkars) from Pakistan's North Western Frontier Province (now called Khyber Pakhtunkhwa) invaded the disputed territory in October, 1947. The Maharaja faced with an internal as well as external invasion, requested the assistance of the Indian armed forces, in return for acceding to India. The Maharaja handed over control of his defences, communication and foreign affairs to the Indian government.

Both sides agreed that the instrument of accession signed by Maharaja Hari Singh be ratified by a referendum, to be held after the hostilities had ceased. Historians on either side of the dispute remained undecided as to whether the Maharaja had signed the document after the Indian troops had entered Kashmir (*i.e.* under duress) or if he did so under no direct military pressure.[1] However, fighting continued through the second half of 1948, with the regular Pakistani army called upon to protect Pakistan's borders ignoring. The war officially ended on January 1, 1949, when the United Nations arranged a ceasefire, with an established ceasefire line, a U.N. Peace keeping force and a recommendation that the referendum on the accession of Kashmir to India be held as agreed earlier.[2] Pakistan controlled roughly one third of the state, referring to it as Azad (free) Kashmir. It is semi autonomous. A larger area including the former kingdom of Hunza and Nagar, are controlled by the central Pakistani government. The Indian side (eastern side) of the ceasefire line is referred to as Jammu and Kashmir state. Both countries refer to the other side of the ceasefire as "occupied" territory.[3]

In 1954, the accession of Jammu and Kashmir to India was ratified by the state's constituent assembly.[4] In 1957, the Jammu and Kashmir constituent assembly approved a constitution. India

[1] An article by Asad Hasim-Kashmir, Timeline On Indo-Pak Rels.in Aljazeera Newspaper.

[2] The Telegaph, 24th September, 2001, A Brief History Of The Kashmir Conflict.

[3] Ibid.

[4] An Article by Asad Hasim-Kashmir-Timeline On Indo-Pak Rels. In AlJazeera Newspaper.

from the point of 1954 ratification and 1957 constitution, begins to refer to Jammu and Kashmir as an integral part of the Indian union. The ceasefire intended to be temporary but the line of control remains the *de facto* border between the two countries.[5] In 1957, Kashmir was formally incorporated into the Indian Union. It was granted a special status under Article 370, of India's constitution, which ensured among other things that non Kashmiri Indians could not buy property there.[6]

Following the 1962 Indo-China War, the foreign ministers of India and Pakistan represented by Swaran Singh and Zulfikar Ali Bhutto respectively, held talks under the auspices of the British and the Americans regarding the Kashmir dispute. The specific contents of those talks are yet to be declassified, but no agreement was reached. In the talks, "Pakistan signified willingness to consider approaches other than a plebiscite and India recognized that the status of Kashmir was in dispute and territorial adjustment might be necessary, according to a declassified US state department memo (dated January 27, 1964)[7] However, following the failure of the 1963 talks, Pakistan referred the Kashmir case to the U.N. Security Council.

In 1965, India fought her second war against Pakistan. The conflict began when the border patrol clashed with their Pakistani counterparts in April in the Rann of Kutch (Gujarat), but it escalated on August 5, 1965 when between 26000 and 33000 Pakistani soldiers dressed as local Kashmiri youths crossed the ceasefire line into India administered Kashmir. Infantry, armour, and air force units were involved in the conflict while it remained localized to the Kashmir theater, but as the war expanded Indian troops crossed the international border at Lahore on September 6, 1965. The largest engagement of the war took place in the Sialkot sector, where between 400 and 600 tanks were squared off in an inconclusive battle.[8]

---

[5] Ibid.
[6] Ibid.
[7] Ibid.
[8] Ibid.

By September 22, 1965, both sides agreed to a U.N. mandated ceasefire, ending the war that had by that point reached a stalemate, with both sides occupying some of each other's territories.[9] On January 10, 1966, the then Prime Minister of India, Lal Bahadur Shastri and the President of Pakistan, Aub Khan signed an agreement at Tashkent (now in Uzbekistan), agreeing to withdraw to their pre-August, 1965 positions and that economic as well as diplomatic relations would be restored. This was known as The Tashkent Agreement.[10]

The full text of the Tashkent Agreement is as follows:

On January 10, 1966, the Prime Minister of India and the President of Pakistan having met at Tashkent and having discussed the existing relations between India and Pakistan, hereby declare their firm resolve to restore normal and peaceful relations between their countries and to promote understanding and friendly relations between their peoples. They consider the attainment of these objectives of vital importance for the welfare of 600 million people of India and Pakistan.

1. The Prime Minister of India and the President Pakistan agreed that both sides will exert all efforts to create good neighborly relation India and Pakistan in accordance the United Nations Charter. They reaffirm their obligation under the Charter not to have recourse to force and settle their disputes through peaceful means. They considered that interests of peace in their region and particularly in the Indo-Pakistan Sub-continent and, indeed in the interests of the people of India and Pakistan were not served by the continuance of tension between the two countries.
2. The Prime Minister of India and the President of Pakistan have agreed that all armed personnel of the two countries shall be withdrawn not later than February 25, 1966 to the positions they held prior to August 5, 1965 and both sides shall observe the ceasefire terms on the ceasefire line.

[9] Ibid.

[10] Government of India, Ministry of External Affairs, declassified Tashkent Agreement Document.

3. The Prime Minister of India and the President of Pakistan have agreed that relations between India and Pakistan shall be based on the principle of non-interference in the internal affairs of each other.
4. The Prime Minister of India and the President of Pakistan have agreed that both sides will discourage propaganda directed against the other country, and will encourage propaganda which promotes the development of friendly relations between the two countries.
5. The Prime Minister of India and the President of Pakistan have agreed that the High Commissioner of India to Pakistan and the High Commissioner of Pakistan to India will return to their posts and that the normal functioning of the diplomatic missions of both countries will be restored. Both governments shall observe the Vienna Convention of 1961 on diplomatic intercourse.
6. The Prime Minister of India and the President of Pakistan have agreed to consider measures towards the restoration of economic and trade relations, communications as well as cultural exchanges between India and Pakistan and to take measures to implement the existing agreements between India and Pakistan.
7. The Prime Minister of India and the President of Pakistan have agreed that they give instructions to their respective authorities to carry out the repatriation of prisoners of war.
8. The Prime Minister of India and the President of Pakistan have agreed that the sides will continue the discussion of questions relating to the problem of refugees and evictions and illegal immigrations. They also agreed that both sides will create conditions which will prevent the exodus of people. They further agreed to discuss the return of the property and assets taken over by either side in connection with the conflict.
9. The Prime Minister of India and the President of Pakistan have agreed that the sides will continue meetings both at the highest and at other levels on matters of direct concern to both countries. Both sides have recognized the need to set up joint Indian-Pakistan bodies which will report to the

Governments in order to decide what further steps should be taken.[11]

Incidentally, another bone of contention between India and Pakistan is the Indus Water Distribution Treaty of 1960, that was brokered by World Bank to use the water available in the Indus System of rivers originating in India, comprising Beas, Sutlej and Ravi. The Pact was signed between India and Pakistan the then Prime Minister of India, Jawharlal Nehru and President of Pakistan, Aub Khan. This was known as The Indus Treaty. This Agreement took nine years of negotiations and divides the control of six rivers between the two nations once signed.[12]

More recently, this Indus River Water Distribution Treaty has become headlines due to the cross border terrorism which has affected India especially Kashmir. Due to the series of terrorist attacks on the Indian subcontinent, the Government of India has threatened to cut off Indus water supply to Pakistan to teach them a lesson but how far it can be done in reality is point to discuss because of international ramifications.

Under this treaty, India got control of Beas, Ravi and Sutlej rivers, while Pakistan got Indus, Chenab and Jhelum rivers. According to this treaty, all waters of the three eastern rivers averaging about 33 million acre feet (MAF) were allocated to India for exclusive use.

Under this Treaty, India On the other hand, the water of the western rivers - Indus, Jhelum and Chenab averaging to around 135 MAF, were allocated to Pakistan except for specific domestic, non-consumptive and agricultural use permitted to India. India has also been given the right to generate hydroelectricity which run through the river projects (ROR), projects on the western rivers, which subject to specific criteria for design and operation is unrestricted.[12A] On the other hand, Indus, Jhelum and Chenab

[11] Ibid. To be noted that in the 1965 war India occupied 1924 sq. kms of Pakistan territory while Pakistan occupied 540 sq.kms of Indian territory.

[12] India Today, February 22, 2019.

[12A] Ibid.

are the lifelines of Pakistan, as the country is highly dependent on these rivers for its water supply. Since these rivers do not originate from Pakistan but flow to the country through India, Pakistan fears the threat of draught and famine. While Jhelum and Chenab originate from India, Indus originates from China, making its way to Pakistan via India.[13] The Treaty clearly spelt the do's and don'ts for both countries; as it allowed India to utilize only 20% of the total water carried by the Indus river. To utilize the waters of the Eastern rivers which have been allocated to India for exclusive use, India has constructed the Bhakra Dam on Sutlej, Pong and Pandoh Dam on Beas and Thein (Ranjitsagar) on Ravi. These storage works, these together with other works Beas-Sutlej link, Madhopur-Beas Link, and Indira Gandhi Nahar Project have helped India utilize nearly the entire share (95%) of the Eastern River waters. However, about two MAF of water annually from Ravi is reported to be still flowing unutilised to Pakistan. To stop the flow of these water, the centre is currently taking three steps-resumption of construction of Shahpurkandi Project, construction of Ujh multipurpose project, and a second Ravi-Beas link.[14]

In 1971, India and Pakistan faced each other for the third time, though, this time, for a different cause, in East Pakistan also known as the Bangladesh war. It is to be noted that the atrocities committed by West Pakistan army and its Urdu speaking Muslims as well as their forceful imposition of Urdu language over the Bengali speaking people of East Pakistan, who demanded recognition of their mother tongue led to a mighty upsurge against West Pakistan. India also in search of creating a buffer territory which would prevent a direct suden attack in the eastern sector as well as to open a second front as till then only a single front was there in the north, India supported the Bangladeshi cause both physically *i.e.* by supplying man, equipment and by providing training and militarily *i.e.* by directly providing military help against Pakistan. This led to the outbreak of the 1971 war in December.

---

[13] Ibid.
[14] Ibid.

The conflict began when the Central Pakistani government in West Pakistan, led by Zulfiqar Ali Bhutto refused to allow the Awami League leader Sheikh Mujibur Rahman, a Bengali speaking person, whose party won majority seats in the 1970 Parliamentary Elections to assume the Premiership.[15]

A Pakistani military crackdown occurred in March, 1971 but India became involved in the conflict in December, after the Pakistani airforce launched a preemptive attack on airfields in India's northwest. India then launched a coordinated land, air and sea assault on East Pakistan. The Pakistani army under Lt. Gen. A.A.K. Niazi surrendered to the Indian army Gen Jagjit Singh Arora at Dhaka whereby more than 90000 Pakistani personnel became prisoners of war. Hostilities lasted for thirteen days only terming it as the shortest war in history.[16] East Pakistan became an independent country and emerged as Bangladesh on December 6, 1971.

Following the end of the war, India, represented by the then Prime Minister of India Mrs. Indira Gandhi and Pakistan by its Prime Minister Zulfiqar Ali Bhutto met at Shimla, Himachal Pradesh, India in 1972 to sign an agreement by which both the countries agreed to put an end to the conflict and confrontation that had so far marred their relations and work for the promotion of a friendly and harmonious relationship and the establishment of a durable peace in the subcontinent. Both sides agreed to settle any dispute by "peaceful means." This was known as the Shimla Agreement of 1972.[17]

The Agreement signed between the two heads of countries on 2nd July, 1972, was much more than a peace treaty seeking to reverse the consequences of the 1971 war (*i.e.* to bring about the withdrawal of troops and an exchange of POWs). It was a comprehensive blue print for neighbhourly relations between India and Pakistan. Under the Shimla Agreement both countries

---

[15] India Today, February 22, 2019.
[16] Ibid.
[17] Ibid.

undertook to abjure conflict and confrontation which had marred relations in the past, and to work towards the establishment of durable peace, friendship and cooperation.[18]

The Shimla Agreement contains a set of guiding principles, mutually agreed to by India and Pakistan, which both sides would adhere to while managing relations with each other. These emphasize: respect for each others' territorial integrity and sovereignty; non interference in each other's internal affairs; respect for each other's unity, political independence; sovereign equality, and abjuring hostile propaganda.

The following principles of the Agreement are, however, particularly noteworthy:

A mutual commitment to the peaceful resolution of all issues through direct bilateral approaches.

To build the foundations of a cooperative relationship with special focus on people to people contacts.

To uphold the inviolability of the Line of Control in Jammu and Kashmir, which is a most CBM between India and Pakistan, and a key to durable peace.

The salient features of the Shimla Agreement are as follows:

1. The Government of India and Government of Pakistan are resolved that the two countries put an end to the conflict and confrontation that have hitherto marred their relations and work for the promotion of a friendly and harmonious relationship and establishment of durable peace in the subcontinent, so that both countries may henceforth devote their resources and energies to the pressing talk of advancing the welfare of their people.
2. In order to achieve this objective, the Government of India and the Government of Pakistan, have agreed as follows:

[18] Government of India, Ministry of External Affairs, Declassified Document, www.govtmea.com.

a. That the principles and purposes of the Charter of the United Nations shall govern the relations between the two countries.

b. That the two countries are resolved to settle their differences by peaceful means through bilateral negotiations or by any other peaceful means mutually agreed upon between them. Pending the final settlement of any of the problems between the two countries, neither side shall unilaterally alter the situation and both shall prevent the organization, assistance or encouragement of any acts detrimental to the maintenance of peaceful and harmonious relations.

c. That the prerequisite for reconciliation, good neighborliness and durable peace between is a commitment by both the countries to peaceful coexistence, respect for each other's territorial integrity, sovereignty and non interference in each other's internal affairs on the basis of equality and mutual benefit.

d. That the basic issues and causes of conflict which have bedevilled the relations between the two countries for the last 25 years shall be resolved by peaceful means.

e. That they should always respect each other's national unity, territorial integrity political independence and sovereign equality.[19]

f. That in accordance with the Charter of the United Nations they will refrain from the threat or the use of force against the territorial integrity or political independence of each other.

3. Both the Governments would take steps within their power to prevent hostile propaganda directed against each other. Both countries would encourage the dissemination of such information as would promote the development of friendly relations between them.

4. In order to progressively restore and normalize relations between the two countries step by step, it was agreed that;

[19] Government of India, Ministry of External Affairs, Declassified Document, govtmea.com

a) steps shall be taken to resume communications, postal, telegraph, sea, land including border posts and air links including overflights.

b) appropriate steps shall be taken to promote travel facilities for the nationals of other countries.

c) trade and cooperation in economic and other agreed fields will be resumed as far as possible.

d) exchange in the fields of science and culture will be promoted.

In this context delegation from the two countries will meet from time to time to work out the necessary details.

5. In order to initiate the process of durable peace, both the governments agreed that:

a) Indian and Pakistani forces should be withdrawn to their side of the international border.

b) In Jammu and Kashmir, the line of control resulting from the ceasefire of December 17, 1971, shall be respected by both sides without any prejudice to the recognized position of either side. Neither side shall seek to alter it unilaterally, irrespective of mutual differences and legal interpretations. Both sides further undertake to refrain from the threat or the use of force in violation of this Line.

6. This Agreement will be subject to ratification by both countries in accordance with their respective constitutional procedures, and will come into force with effect from the date on which the Instrument of Ratification are exchanged.

7. Both Governments agreed that their respective Heads will meet again at a mutually convenient time in the future and that in the meanwhile the representatives of the two sides will meet to discuss further the modalities and arrangements for the establishment of durable peace and normalization of relations including the question of repatriation of prisoners of war and civilian internees, a final settlement of Jammu and Kashmir and the resumption of diplomatic relations.[20]

Thus, the Shimla Agreement designated the ceasefire line December 17, 1971 as being the new Line of Control (LOC)

[20] Government of India, Ministry of External Affairs, Declassified Document.

between the two countries, which neither side seeks to alter unilaterally, and "which shall be respected by both sides without prejudice to the recognized position of either side.

In 1974, the Kashmiri state government affirmed that "the state is a constituent unit of the Union of India." Pakistan rejected the accord with the Government of India. On May 18, 2019, the Indian government detonated a nuclear device at Pokharan, in an operation named "Smiling Buddha". India referred to the device as a peaceful nuclear explosive.[21]

In 1988, the two countries signed an agreement that neither side would attack the other's nuclear installations. These included "nuclear power and research reactors, fuel fabrication, uranium enrichment, isotopes separation and reprocessing facilities as well as any other installation with fresh or irradiated nuclear fuel and materials in any form and establishments storing significant quantities of radioactive materials." Both sides agreed to share information on the latitudes and longitudes of all nuclear installations. This agreement was later ratified and the two countries share information on January 1, each year since then.[22]

From 1989, upsurge against the centre began to break out in Kashmir and first signs of armed resistance to Indian rule in the Kashmir valley could be seen. Muslim political parties after accusing the state government of rigging in the 1987 state legislative elections, formed activist wings. Pakistan said it would give its moral and diplomatic support to the movement, reiterating its call for the earlier UN sponsored referendum. India said that Pakistan was supporting the resistance by providing weapons and training to fighters, terming attacks against it in Kashmir as "cross border terrorism. " But Pakistan denied this.[23]

Activist groups taking part in the fight in Kashmir continued to emerge through the 1990s, in part fuelled by a large influx of

[21] An Article by Asad Hashim-Indo-Pak Rels, A Time Line, AlJazeera Newspaper.
[22] Ibid.
[23] An Article by Asad Hashim-Indo-Pak Rels.-A Time Line in AlJazeera Newspaper.

"mujahideen" who took part in the Afghan war against the Soviets in the 1980s.[24]

In 1991, the two countries signed an agreement on providing advance notification of military exercises, manoeuvres and troop movements, as well as preventing airspace violations and establishing overflight rules.[25]

In 1992, a joint declaration prohibiting the use of chemical weapons was signed in New Delhi. However, a series of clashes since 1995, military officials of both countries met at the LOC to ease tensions.[26]

In 1998, India detonated five nuclear devices at Pokharan. Pakistan responded by detonating six nuclear devices of its own in the Chaghai Hills. The tests resulted in sanctions being placed on both countries. In the same year both countries carried out tests of long range missiles.[27]

In 1999, the then Indian Prime Minister Atal Behari Vajpayee met with Nawaz Sharif, his Pakistani counterpart, in Lahore. The two signed the Lahore Declaration, the first major agreement between the two countries since the 1972 Shimla Accord. Both countries reaffirmed their commitment to the Shimla Accord, and agreed to undertake a number of 'Confidence Building Measures' (CBMs)[28]

The Lahore Declaration was signed on February 2, 1999. The following is the text of the Lahore Declaration:

Sharing a vision of text and stability between their countries, and of progress and prosperity for their peoples.

Convinced that durable peace and development of harmonious relations and friendly cooperation would serve the vital interests

[24] Ibid.
[25] Ibid.
[26] Ibid.
[27] Ibid.
[28] Ibid.

of the peoples of the two countries, enabling them to devote their energies for a better future.

Recognizing the nuclear dimension of the security environment of the two countries added to their responsibility for avoidance of conflict between the two countries.

Committed to the principles and purposes of the Charter of the United Nations, and the universally accepted principles of coexistence.

Reiterate the determination of both countries to implementing the Shimla Agreement in letter and spirit. Committed to the objective of universal nuclear disarmament and non proliferation;

Convinced of the importance of mutually agreed confidence building measures for improving the security environment.

Recalling their agreement of 23rd September, 1998, that an environment of peace and security in the supreme national interest of both sides and that the resolution of all outstanding issues, including Jammu and Kashmir, is essential for this purpose.

Have agreed that their respective governments:

Shall intensify their efforts to resolve all issues including Jammu and Kashmir.

Shall refrain from intervention and interference in each other's internal affairs.

Shall intensify composite and integrated dialogue process for an early and positive outcome of the agreed bilateral agenda.

Shall take immediate steps for reducing the risk of accidental or unauthorised of nuclear weapons and discuss concepts and doctrines with a view to elaborating measures for confidence building in the nuclear and conventional fields, aimed at prevention of conflict.

Reaffirm their commitment to the goals and objectives of the SAARC and to concert their efforts towards the realization of the

SAARC vision for the future with view to promoting the welfare of the peoples of south Asia and to improve their quality of life through accelerated economic, social progress and cultural development.

Reaffirm their condemnation of terrorism in all its forms and manifestations and their determination to combat this menace.

Shall promote and protect all human rights and fundamental freedoms.

On February 21,1999, a Memorandum of Understanding was signed between the Foreign Secretary of India, K. Raghunath and the Foreign Secretary of Pakistan, Mr. Shamshad Ahmad in Lahore, which is the following:

Reaffirming their continued commitment to respective governments the determination of both the countries to implementing the Shimla Agreement in letter and spirit. Guided by the agreement between the Prime Ministers 23rd September, 1998, that an environment of peace and security is the supreme national interest of both sides and that resolution of all outstanding issues including Jammu and Kashmir is essential for this purpose.

Pursuant to the directive given by the respective Prime Ministers in Lahore, to adopt measures for promoting a stable environment of peace and security between the two countries.

Further, they agreed:

The two sides shall engage in bilateral consultations on security concepts and nuclear doctrines with a view to developing measures for confidence building in the nuclear and conventional fields aimed at avoidance of conflict.

The two sides undertake to provide each other with advance notification in respect of ballistic missile flight tests and shall conclude a bilateral agreement in this regard.

The two sides are fully committed to undertaking national measures to reducing the risks of accidental and unauthorized use of nuclear weapons under their respective control. The two sides further undertake to notify each other immediately in the event of any accidental, unauthorized or unexplained incident that could create the risk of a fall out with adverse consequences for both sides, or an outbreak of a nuclear war between the two countries, as well as to adopt measures aimed at diminishing the the possibility of such actions or such incidents being misinterpreted by the other. The two sides shall identify/establish the appropriate communication mechanism for this purpose.

The two sides shall continue to abide by their respective unilateral moratorium on conducting further nuclear test explosions unless either side, in exercise of its national sovereignty decides that extraordinary events have jeopardized its supreme interests.

The two sides should conclude an agreement on prevention of incidents at sea in order to ensure safety of navigation by naval vessels, and aircraft belonging to the two sides.

The two sides should periodically review the implementation of existing Confidence Building Measures (CBMs) and where necessary, set up appropriate consultative mechanisms to monitor and ensure effective implementation of these CBMs.

The two sides should undertake a review of the existing communication links (*e.g.* between the respective Director-General, military operations) with a view to upgrading and improving these links, and to provide for fail-safe and secure communications.

The two sides should engage in bilateral consultations on security and disarmament and non proliferation issues within the context of negotiations on these issues in multilateral fora.

Where required the technical details of the above measures would be worded out by experts of the two sides in meetings to be held on mutually agreed dates, before mid 1999, with a view to reaching bilateral agreements.

This Declaration was signed in the backdrop of Delhi-Lahore Bus service which was inaugurated earlier in 1999.[29]

Despite the above Agreements and Confidence Building Measures, clandestinely the Pakistani army was planning to infiltrate into India, thus preparing the ground for a major conflagration much unknown to India. It is a fact that during winter time, due to sever cold, the soldiers come down to the lower altitude leaving the bunkers empty in the higher regions. Taking this advantage the Pakistani army, the Northern Light Infantry in the guise of locals along with their sponsored terrorists began to occupy those bunkers, thus gaining a height advantage overlooking the NH-1, which connects Jammu and Kashmir especially Ladakh region with the rest of India. Now, these infiltrators threatened to cut off this lifeline. But strangely, the Indian Army Intelligence failed to gather this information. It was the local Gujjars who took their domestic animals to graze in the upper heights informed the army when already the army had lost quite a few of its men. This led to what was known as Kargil conflict, which took place between May and July, 1999 in Jammu and Kashmir's Kargil district.

The conflict was believed to have been orchestrated by the then Pakistan army chief, Genera Pervez Musharraf might be without the knknowledge of Pakistan Prime Minister Nawaz Sharif. Based on information provided by the local shepherds, the Indian army was able to ascertain the points of incursion and launched "Operation Vijay". The army declared the mission successful on July 26, 1999. But the victory came at a high price. The official death toll on the Indian side was 527, while that on the Pakistani side was 357 and 453. In the war Pakistan shot down two Indian fighter jets while another fighter jet crashed during the operation. Pakistan asked the United States to intervene but the then US President Bill Clinton refused until Pakistan withdrew their army beyond the Line of Control. As Pakistani troops withdrew, the Indian army attacked the rest of the outposts managing to get

[29] Government of India, Ministry of External Affairs, www.govtmea.com

them back, the last being on July 26, 1999. Pakistan initially denied the role of their army in the conflict, saying India was facing off the Kashmiri freedom fighters. But, when later, their soldiers were awarded medals for their roles in the conflict, all doubts about Pakistan army involvement were removed.[30] Below are some glimpses of Kargil conflict:

Since the Kargil war, tensions along the LOC remained high, and in 2001, 38 people were killed in an attack on the Kashmiri Assembly in Srinagar. Following that attack, the then Chief Minister of Jammu and Kashmir, Farooq Abdullah called on the Indian government to launch a full scale military operation against alleged terrorist training camps in Pakistan.[31]

In July, 2001, Pakistani President Pervez Musharraf and the Indian Prime Minister Atal Behari Vajpayee met for a two day summit at Agra. That summit collapsed after two days with no sides being able to come to an agreement on the core issue of Kashmir, though Musharraf suggested that LOC be converted into international border.[32]

On December 13, 2001, an armed attack on the Indian Parliament in New Delhi left fourteen people dead. India blamed Lashkar-eTaiba and Jaish-e-Mohammed for the attacks. This led to the amassing of troops on both sides of the LOC. The standoff ended in October, 2002, after international mediation.[33]

In 2002, President Musharraf pledged that Pakistan would combat extremism on it's own soil, but affirmed that the country had a right to Kashmir.

In 2003, after Musharraf called for a ceasefire along the LOC, during a UN General Assembly meeting in September, the two

---

[30] The Economic Times, 28th July, 2018.

[31] An Article by Asad Hashimi-Indo-Pak Relations, A Timeline, in AlJazeera Newspaper.

[32] Ibid.

[33] An Article by Asad Hashimi-Indo-Pak Relations, A Timeline in AlJazeera Newspaper.

countries reached an agreement to cool tensions and cease hostilities across the defacto border.[34]

In 2004, Vajpayee and Musharraf held direct talks at the 12th SAARC Summit in Islamabad, January, and the two countries' foreign secretaries met later in the year. That year marked the beginning of Composite Dialogue Process, in which bilateral meetings were held between officials at various levels of government (including foreign ministers, foreign secretaries, military officers, border security officials, anti-narcotic officials and nuclear experts). In November, on the eve of a visit to Indian administered Kashmir, the New Indian Prime Minister Monmohan Singh, announced that India would be reducing its deployment of troops there. In 2006, India redeployed 5000 troops from Jammu and Kashmir, citing an improvement in the situation there, but the two countries were unable to reach an agreement on withdrawing forces from the Siachen Glacier.[35]

In September 2006, President Musharraf and Prime Minister Singh agreed to put into place an India-Pakistan institutional anti-terrorism mechanism.[36]

On February 18, 2007, the Samjhauta Express, which started its journey on 22nd July, 1976 as a daily train but later changed to biweekly Express in 1994, was bombed near Panipat, New Delhi, whereby 68 people were killed and dozens injured. At the same time the fifth round of talks regarding the review of nuclear and ballistic missile related CBMs was held as part of the Composite Dialogue Process. The second round of Joint Anti-Terrorism Mechanism (JATM) was also held.[37]

In 2008, India joined a framework agreement between Turkmenistan, Afghanistan and Pakistan on a $7.6 bn gas pipeline project. A series of Kashmir specific CBMs were also agreed to

[34] Ibid.
[35] Ibid.
[36] An Article by Asad Hashimi-Indo-Pak Relations, Timeline in AlJazeera Newspaper.
[37] Ibid.

(including the approval of a triple entry permit facility). In July, 2008, India blamed the Pakistan's Inter Service Intelligence (ISI) directorate for a bomb attack on the Indian Embassy at Kabul, which killed 58 and injured another 141. In September, 2008, Pakistani President Asif Ali Zardari and Indian Prime Minister Monmohan Singh formally announced the opening of several trade routes between the two countries. In October, 2008, cross-LoC trade commenced though it was limited to 21 items and could take place on only two days a week.[38] In November 26, 2008, armed gunmen opened fire on civilians at several sites in Mumbai, India. The attacks on the Taj Mahal Palace and Tower, the Oberoi Trident Hotel, the Chhatrapati Shivaji Terminus, Leopold Cafe, Cama Hospital, Nariman House Jewish Community Center, Metro Cinema, St. Xavier's College, and in a lane near the Times of India office, prompted an almost three day siege of the Taj, where gunmen remained holed up until all but one of them were killed in a Indian Security Force operation. More than 160 people were killed in the attack.[39]

In this context, Ajmal Kasab, the only attacker captured alive, told the police that the attackers were members of Lashkar-eTaiba. In the wake of the attacks, India broke off talks with Pakistan.[40]

In 2009, The Pakistani Government admitted that the Mumbai attacks might have been partly planned on Pakistani soil, while vigorously denying allegations that the plotters were sanctioned or aided by Pakistan's intelligence agencies. Pakistani Prime Minister Yusuf Raja Gilani and Indian Prime Minister Manmohan Singh met on the sidelines of a non-aligned movement (NAM) summit Sharm-el-Sheikh, Egypt issued a joint statement charting future talks. Singh ruled out, however, the resumption of the Composite Dialogue Process at that time. The Indian government continue to take a stern line with Pakistan, however, with its coalition government saying that it was up to Pakistan to take the

[38] Ibid.

[39] Ibid.

[40] An Article by Asad Hashimi-Indo-Pak Relations,Timeline in AlJazeera Newspaper.

first step towards the resumption of substantive talks by cracking down the activist groups on its soil. In August, 2009, India gave Pakistan a new dossier of evidence regarding Mumbai attacks, asking it to prosecute Hafeez Mohammmed Saeed, the Head of Jamaat-u-dawa, a Islamic charity with ties to Lashkar-eTaiba.[41]

In 2010, January, Pakistani and Indian forces exchanged fire across the LOC in Kashmir which gave rise to tension in the area. In February, 2010, India and Pakistan's foreign secretaries met in New Delhi for talks. This was followed by the two countries' foreign ministers' meeting in Islamabad in July. In May, Ajmal Kasab was found guilty of murder, conspiracy, and of waging war against India in the Mumbai attacks case. He was sentenced to death.[42]

In January 2011, Indian Home Secretary G. K. Pillai commented that India would share information about 2001 Samjhauta Express bombing case. The two countries' foreign secretaries met at Thimpu, Bhutan in February and agreed to resume peace talks on all issues.[43]

In November, 2012, India executed Pakistani national Kasab, the lone survivor of a fighter squad that killed 166 people in a rampage through the financial capital Mumbai in 2008, hanging him just days before the fourth anniversary of the attack.[44]

In January, 2013 India and Pakistan traded accusations of violating the ceasefire in Kashmir, with Islamabad accusing Indian troops of a cross-border raid that killed a soldier and India charging that Pakistani shelling had destroyed a home on its side. In September, the same year the Prime Ministers of India and Pakistan met in New York on the sidelines of the UN General Assembly. Both the leaders agreed to end tension between armies of both sides in the disputed Kashmir.[45]

---

[41] Ibid.
[42] Ibid.
[43] Ibid.
[44] Ibid.
[45] An Article by Asad Hashimi-Indo-Pak Relations, Timeline in AlJazeera Newspaper.

On February 12, 2014, India and Pakistan agreed to release trucks held in their respective territories, ending a three week impasse triggered by the seizure of a truck in India administered Kashmir coming from across the defacto Line of Control allegedly carrying brown sugar. On 1st May, 2014, Pakistan's Army Chief General Raheel Sharif called Kashmir the "jugular vein of Pakistan and that the dispute should be resolved in accordance with wishes and aspirations of Kashmiris in line with the UNSC Resolutions for lasting peace in the region.[46]

On May 25, 2014, Pakistan released 151 Indian fishermen from its jails in a goodwill gesture ahead of the swearing-in ceremony of Narendra Modi as Prime Minister of India. On May 27, 2014, Indian Prime Minister Narendra Modi held talks with Pakistan's Prime Minister Nawaz Sharif in New Delhi. Both sides expressed willingness to begin a new era of bilateral relations.[47]

In 2015, Prime Minister Modi made a surprise visit to the Pakistani Eastern City of Lahore on Sharif 's birthday and the wedding of his grand daughter.[48]

However, all these goodwill gestures and confidence building measures had no impact on the Pakistani army, their Inter Service Intelligence and terrorists as from 2016 to 2019, the Pakistan sponsored terrorist organizations led severe strikes against Indian military personnel first at Pathankot, then Uri and lastly Pulwama. In the last case more than 49 Indian military personnel were killed by a suicide car bombing in the military convoy in 2019. This resulted in two surgical strikes as a last resort by India - the first one in Pok and the last one, an air strike deep inside Pakistan. At the present moment as a consequence of this there is a stalemate in India-Pakistan relations. This brings us to the question of rise of terrorism in the world and Kashmir valley which is discussed in the next chapter.

---

[46] Ibid.
[47] Ibid.
[48] Ibid.

5

RISE OF WORLD TERRORISM

Terrorism is usually understood as the use or threat of violence to further a political cause. There is no universally agreed definition of terrorism making it a difficult to quantify. Scholars agree that terrorism is a disputed term and very few those labeled terrorists described themselves as such. Depending how broadly the term is defined, the roots and practice of terrorism could be traced back to the 1st century A.D. Therefore, terrorism is not a 21st century phenomenon and has its roots in early resistance and political movements. The Sicarii were an early terrorist organization founded in the 1st century A.D. with the goal of overthrowing the Romans in the Middle East. Judas of Galilee, leader of the zealots and a key influence on the Sicarii, believed that the Jews should be ruled by God alone and that armed resistance was necessary.[1]

Unlike the zealots, the Sicariis targeted other Jews they believed to be collaborators or traitors to the cause. The tactics used by the Sicarii were detailed by the historian Josephus in 50 A.D.: "they would mingle with the crowd, carrying short dagger concealed under their clothing, with which they stabbed their enemies. Then when they fell, the murderers would join in the

[1] Terrorism by Max Roser, Mohammed Nagdy and Hannah Ritchie.

cries of indignation and through this plausible behavior, avoided discovery.[2]

The first use in English of the term "terrorism" occurred during the French Revolution's Reign of Terror, when the Jacobins, who ruled the revolutionary state, employed violence, including mass executions by guillotine, to compel obedient to the state and intimidate regime enemies.[3] In the mid nineteenth century the term terrorism began to be associated with non governmental groups. Anarchism, often in league with rising nationalism and anti monarchist was the most prominent ideology associated with terrorism.[4]

In the 20th century, terrorism continued to be associated with a vast array of anarchist, socialist fascists and nationalist groups, many of them engaged in 'third world' anti colonial struggles. Some scholars also labeled as terrorist the systematic internal violence and intimidation practised by states such as the Stalinist Soviet Union and Nazi Germany.[5]

In the 11th century, the Hashshashin (a. k. a. the Assassins) arose, an offshoot of the Ismaili sect of Shia Muslims.[6] Led by Hassan-i Sabbah and opposed to the Fatimid rule, the Hashshashin militia seized Alamut and other fortress strongholds across Persia.[7] The Hashshashin forces were too small to challenge militarily, so they assassinated city governors, and military commanders in order to create alliances with militarily powerful neighbours. The Hashshashin also carried out assassinations as

---

[2] Richard A Horsley-"The Sicarii, Ancient Jewish Terrorists, The Journal of Religion (1979), pp. 435–458.

[3] Francois Furstenberg-"Opinion, Bush's Dangerous Liaisons", 28th October, 2007, www.NY Times.com.

[4] Ibid.

[5] Martin A Miller-The Foundation of Modern Terrorism: State, Society and the Dynamics of Political Violence, Cambridge University Press, p.

[6] David Rapoport-"Fear And Trembling": Terrorism In Three Religious Traditions, American Political Science Review, 1984, p. 658.

[7] Ibid.

retribution.[8] The sons of liberty was a clandestine society that was formed in Boston and New York city in the 1770s. It had a political agenda of independence of Britain's American colonies. The groups engaged in several acts that could be considered terroristic and used the deeds for propaganda purposes.[9]

On November 5, 1605, a group of conspirators led by Robert Catesby atttempted to destroy the English Parliament on its State Opening by King James I. They planned in secret to detonate a large quantity gunpowder placed beneath the Palace of Westminister. The gunpowder was procured and placed by Guy Fawkes. The group intended to enact a coup detat by killing James I, and the members of both houses of Parliament. The conspirators planned to make one of the King's children a puppet monarch and then restore the Catholic faith to England.

The conspirator leased a coal cellar beneath the house of Lords and began stockpiling gunpowder in 1604. As well as its primary targets, it would have killed hundreds, if not thousands of Londoners - the most devastating act of terrorism in the history of Britain plunging the nation into a religious war. English spymasters uncovered the plot and caught Guy Fawkes with the gunpowder beneath Parliament. This planned attack had been known as the Gunpowder Plot. It is often compared with modern religious terrorism such as the attacks on the twin towers in the U.S. by Islamic terrorists on 9/11, 2001.[10] In the 19th century, powerful stable and affordable explosives were developed, global integration reached unprecedented levels and often radical political movements became widely influential.[11]

---

[8] Marshal G.S. Hodgson: The Secret Order of Assassins, The Struggle of the Early Nizari Ismaili against the Islamic World, University of Pennsylvania Press, p. 83

[9] Ibid.

[10] Antonia Fraser-The Gunpowder Plot: Terror and Faith in 1605, Weidenfield and Nicolson. Also, in www.telegraph.co.uk-an article published by Nick Britten (21st April, 2005).

[11] Gerard Chalian-The History of Terrorism: From Antiquity To al Qaeda. Berkeley: University of California Press, 2007, p. 124.

One of the earliest groups to utilize modern terrorist techniques was arguably the Fenian Brotherhood ad its offshoot the Irish Republican Brotherhood. They were both founded in 1858 as revolutionary, militant nationalist and Catholic groups, both in Ireland and amongst the emigre community in the United States.[12]

After centuries of continued British rule, and influenced most recently from the devastating effects of the 1840s Irish Potato Famine, these revolutionary fraternal organizations were founded with the aim of establishing an independent republic in Ireland, and began carrying out frequent acts of violence in metropolitan Britain to achieve their aims through intimidation.[13]

The concept of "propaganda of the deed" advocated physical violence or other provocative public acts against political enemies in order to inspire mass rebellion or revolution. One of the first individuals associated with this concept, the Italian revolutionary, Carlo Pisacane (1818–1857), wrote in his "Political Testament" (1857), that ideas spring from deeds and not the other way round. By the 1880s, the slogan, "propaganda of the deed" had begun to be used to refer to bombings, regicide and tyrannicides.[14]

Founded in Russia in 1858, Narodnya Volya (His book People's Will in English) was a revolutionary anarchist group. Inspired by Sergei Nechayev and by "propaganda by the deed", theorist Pisacane. Individual Europeans also engaged in politically motivated violence. Prior to the American Civil War, abolitionist John Brown (1800–1859) advocated and practised armed opposition slavery, leading several attacks between 1856 and 1859, the most of them being launched in 1859 against the armory at Harpers Ferry. After the civil war on December 24, 1865, six Confederate veterans created the Ku Klu Klux. The KKK used violence, lynching, murder and acts of intimidation such as cross burning to oppress African Americans in particular, and it created

[12] Richard-Irish Freedom, English Publisher, Pan Books, 2nd November, 2007, p. 180.

[13] Ibid.

[14] Anarchism, A Documentary History of Libertarian Ideas.

a sensation with its masked forays dramatic nature.[15] The groups politics were white supremacists, anti semitic racist, anti Catholic and nativist.

Several nationalist groups used violence against an Ottoman Empire in apparent decline. One was the Armenian Revolutionary Federation, revolutionary movement founded in Tiflis (Russian Trascaucasia) in 1890 by Christapor Mikaelian. The group used to publish newspapers, smuggle arms, hijack buildings as it sought to bring in European intervention that would force the Ottoman to surrender control of its Armenian territories.[16] Also inspired by the Narodnya Volya, the internal Macedonian Revolutionary Organization (IMRO) was a revolutionary movement founded in 1893 by Hristo Tatarchev in the Ottoman controlled Macedonian territories. Through assassinations and by provoking uprisings, the group sought to coerce the Ottoman government into creating a Macedonian nation.[17]

The use of terrorism to further the political cause has accelerated in recent years. Modern terrorism largely came in to being after the second world war with the rise of the nationalist movements in the old empires of European powers. These early anti-colonial movements in the old empires of the European powers recognized the ability of terrorism to generate publicity for the cause and influence of global policy. Bruce Hoffman, director of the centre for security studies at George Town University, wrote that "The ability of these groups to mobilize sympathy and support outside the narrow confines of actual theatres of operation thus taught a powerful lesson to the similarly aggrieved peoples elsewhere, who now saw in terrorism an effective means of transforming hitherto local conflicts into international issues. This development paved the way for international terrorism in the 1960s.[18]

---

[15] Jackson, 1992 edited, pp. 241–242.

[16] Gerard Chalian-The History of Terrorism: From Antiquity To al Qaeda, Berkeley, University of California Press, 2007, p. 193.

[17] Ibid.

[18] Bruce Hoffman-Inside Terrorism, Columbia University Press, 2013.

However, revolutionary nationalism continued to motivate political violence in the 20th century, much of it directed against western colonial powers. The Irish Republican Army campaigned against the British in 1910s and after years of warfare, London agreed to the 1921 Anglo-Irish Treaty creating a free Irish state encompassing 26 of the island's 32 countries.[19] This movement inspired the Zionist groups, Hagannah, Irgun and Lehi to fight the British throughout the 1930s in the Palestine Mandate.[19] Like the IRA and the Zionist groups, the Muslim Brotherhood in Egypt used bombings and assassinations to try to free territory from British control.[20]

The Womems' Suffrage Movement in the U.K. also committed terrorist attacks prior to the first world war. There were three phases of WSPU militancy in 1905, 1908 and 1913; including civil disobedience, destruction of public property and arson and bombings.[21]

Political assassinations continued, resulting in the assassinations of King Umberto I of Italy, killed in July 1900, and US President William McKinley September 1901. Political violence became especially widespread in Imperial Russia and several ministers were killed in the opening years of the 20th century.[22]

On June 28, 1914, Gabrilo Princip one of a group of six assassins, shot and killed Archduke Franz Ferdinand of Austria and his wife Sophie, Duchess of Hohenberg in Sarajevo, the capital of Condominium of Bosnia and Herzegovina. The assassination produced widespread shock across Europe setting in motion a series of events leading to the first world war.[23]

---

[19] Tim Coogan, Michael Collins-The Man Who Made Ireland, New York, Palgrave MacMillan, 2002, p. 92.

[20] Brynjar Lia-The Society of the Muslim Brothers in Egypt; The Rise of an Islamic Mass Movement, Ithaca Press, 2006, p. 53. Also, J. Bowyer Bell-Terror Out of Zion; Irgun Zvai Leumi-Lehi And The Palestine Underground, 1929–49, Avon, 1985, p. 14.

[21] Peter Rowland-David Lloyd George: a Biography, 1978, MacMillan, p. 228.

[22]. Fontanja 16-The Tsar's Secret Police by Charles A Ruud, Sergei A Stepanov.

[23] Ibid.

In the 1930s, the Nazi Germany and the Stalin's rule in Soviet Union practised state terror systematically and on a massive and unprecedented scale. Meanwhile, Stalin's regime branded its opponents with the label 'terrorists'.[24]

Following the 1929 Hebron massacre of 67 Jews in the British Mandate of Palestine, the Zionist militia Haganah transformed itself into a paradi force. In 1931, however, the more militant Irgun broke away from Haganah, objecting to Haganag's policy of restraint. After the British in the White Paper of 1939, placed severe restrictions on Jewish immigration into Palestine and set forth the vision of a single state with an Arab majority, the Irgun began a campaign against British rule by assassinating police, capturing British government buildings and arms and sabotaging British railways.[25] Some of the tactics of guerrilla, partisan and resistance movements organized and supplied by the allies during wwII, according to historian M.R.D. Foot, can be considered terrorist.[26]

After World War II, largely successful anti colonial campaigns were launched against the collapsing European empires, as many World War II resistance groups became militantly anti colonial. The Viet Minh, *e.g.*, which had fought against the Japanese, now fought against the returning French colonists. In the Middle East, the Muslim Brotherhood used bombings and assassinations against British rule in Egypt.[27]

Also, during the 1950s, the National Liberation Front (FLN) in French controlled Algeria and the EOKA in British controlled Cyprus waged guerrilla and open war against colonial wars.[28] In the 1960s, inspired by Mao's Chinese Revolution of 1949 and

[24] Ibid.
[25] Howard Sachar-A History of Israel: From The Rise of Zionism To Our Times, New York, Knopf, 2007, p. 247.
[26] M.R.D. Foot-Resistance, An Analysis of European Resistance To Nazism, 1940–45.
[27] Brynjar Lia-The Society of Muslim Brothers in Egypt: The Rise of an Islamic Mass Movement, 1928–42, Ithaca Press, 2006, p. 53.
[28] Hoffman-1998, p. 33.

Castro's Cuban Revolution of 1959, national independence movements often fused nationalist and socialist impulses. This was the case with Spain's ETA, the Front de la liberation du Quebec, and the Palestine Liberation Organization.[29]

In the late 1960s and 1970s violent left wing and revolutionary groups were on the rise, sympathizing with third world guerrilla movements and seeking to spark anti-capitalist revolts. Such groups included the PKK in Turkey, Armenia's ASALA, the Japanese Red Army, the German Red Army Faction, the Italian Red Brigade, and in the United States, the Weather Underground.

Nationalist groups such as the Provisional IRA and the Tamil Tigers also began operations at this time.[30]

Throughout the Cold War, both the United States and Soviet Union made extensive use of violent nationalist organizations to carry on a war by proxy. For example, Soviet and Chinese military advisers provided training and support to the Viet Cong. during the Vietnam War.[31] The Soviet Union also provided military support to the PLO during the Israeli-Palestinian conflict and Fidel Castro during the Cuban Revolution. The United States funded groups such as the Contras in Nicaragua. Many violent Islamic militants of the 20th century had been funded in the 1980s by the United States and the U.K. because they were fighting the USSR in Afghanistan.[32]

Fatah was organized as a Palestinian Nationalist Group in 1954, and exists today as a political party in Palestine. In 1967, it joined the Palestine Liberation Organization for secular Palestinian National Groups formed in 1964. The PLO began its own armed operations in 1965.[33] The PLO's membership comprised separate

[29] Gerard Chaliand-The History of Terrorism: From Antiquity to al Qaeda, Berekeley, University of California Press, 2007, p. 227.
[30] Amy Zalman-Where did left wing terrorism go? About.com, News and Issues.
[31] Stanley Karnow-Vietnam: A History, 1983.
[32] George Crile-Charlie Wilson's War, Atlantic Monthy Press, pp. 111-112.
[33] Barry Rubin-Revolution Until Victory? The Politics and History of the PLO., Harvard University Press, 196, p. 7.

and possibly contending paramilitary and political factions, the largest of which included Fatah, the Popular Front For The Liberation of Palestine (PFLP) and the Democratic Front For The Liberation of Palestine (DFLP).[34]

The People's Mujahedeen of Iran (PMOI) or Mujahedeen e Khalq (founded in 1965), is a socialist Islamic group that has fought Iran's government since the Khomeini Revolution. The group originated to oppose capitalism and what it perceived as western exploitation of Iran under the Shah. The group would go on to play an important role in the Shah's overthrow but was unable to capitalize on this in the power-vacuum. The group is suspected to have a membership between 10000 and 30000. The group renounced violence in 2001 but remained a proscribed terror organization in Iran and the US. The EU however, has removed the group from its terror list.[35]

In 1975, Hagop Tarachian and Hagop Hagopian, with the help of sympathetic Palestinians, founded the Armenian Secret Army for the Liberation of Armenia (ASALA) in Beirut during the Lebanese Civil War. At the time Turkey was in political turmoil and Hagopian believed that the time was right to avenge the Armenians who died during the Armenian Genocide and to force the Turkish Government to cede the territory of Wilsonian Armenia to establish a nation state also incorporating the Armenian SSR.[36]

The "Partiya Karkaren Kurdistan" (Kurdistan Workers Party or PKK) was established in Turkey in 1978 as a Kurdish Nationalist Party. Founder Abdullah Ocalan was inspired by the Maoist Theory of People's War and like Algeria's FLN advocated the use of compliance terror. The group sought to create an independent Kurdish state consisting parts of south-eastern Turkey, north-eastern Iraq, north-eastern Syria and north-western Iran. In 1984, the PKK transformed itself into a paramilitary organization and

[34] Hoffman-1998, p. 47.

[35] The Iran Primer-"US Terrorism Report: MEK and Jundallah.

[36] Olivier Roy-Turkey Today, A European NATO, London, Anthem Press, Press, p. 170.

launched conventional attacks as well as bombings against Turkish governmental installations.[37]

In Europe, founded in 1959, and functioning until 2018, the Euskadi Ta Askatasuna (or ETA- "Basque for Basque Homeland and Freedom", was an armed Basque nationalist separatist organization. Formed in response to the suppression of the Basque language and culture under the regime of General Francis Franco (in power 1939–75), in Spain, ETA evolved from an advocacy group for traditional Basque culture into an armed Marxist group demanding Basque independence.[38]

The Provisional Irish Republican Army (IRA) was an Irish Nationalist Movement founded in December, 1969, when several militants, including Sean Mac Stioain, broke off from the official IRA and formed a new organization. Led by Mac Stiofain in the early 1970s and by a group led by Gerry Adams since the late 1970s, the Provisional IRA sought to bring about an all-island Irish state. On July 21, 1972, the group in an attack later dubbed as Black Friday, set off twenty two bombs, killing nine and injuring 130. Earlier, they during a period known as the Troubles, the group conducted an armed campaign, including bombings, gun attacks, assassinations and even a mortar attack on 10 Downing Street. On July 28, 2005, the Provisional IRA Army Council announced an end to its armed campaign.[39]

The Red Army Faction (RAF) was a New Left group, founded in 1968 by Andreas Badder and Ulrike Meinhoff in West Germany. Inspired by Che Guevara, Maoist Socialism and the Vietcong, the group sought to raise awareness of the Vietnamese and Palestinian independence movement through kidnappings, taking embassies hostage, bank robberies, assassinations, bombings and attacks on US air bases.[40] The Front de Liberation du Quebec (FLQ) was a

[37] Scott Peterson-"Turkish Kurds: Some Back The State"

[38] Mark, Kurlansky-The Basque History of the World: The Story of a Nation, New York, Penguin, 2001, p. 224.

[39] Chaliand, p. 251 & Coogan, p. 356.

[40] Bernhard Blumenau-"The United Nations and Terrorism. Germany, multilateralism, and Terrorism Efforts in the 1970s, " Palgrave MacMillan, 2014, Ch-1.

Marxist Nationalist group that sought to create an independent Quebec. George's Schoeters founded the group in 1963 and was inspired by Che Guevara and Algeria's FLN. The group was accused of bombings, kidnappings, and assassinations of politicians, soldiers and civilians.[41]

In Colombia, several paramilitary and guerrilla groups were formed during the 1960s and afterwards. Paramilitary groups associated with narcoterrorism include the Ejercito de Liberacion National (ELN), the Fyerzas Armadas Revolucionarius de Colombia (AUC). While the ELN and FARC were originally left wing revolutionary groups, all had conducted numerous attacks on civilians and civilian infrastructure and engaged in the drug trade. The US and some European governments consider them terrorist organisation.[42]

The Jewish Defense League (JDL) was founded in 1969 by the Rabbi Meir Kahane in New York City with its declared purpose being the protection of the jews from harassment and antisemitism. The National Consortium for the Study of Terror and Responses to Terrorism stated that during the JDL's first two decades of activity, it was an active terrorist organization.[43] The Fuerzas Armadas de Liberacion Nacional (FALN - Armed forces National Liberation) is a nationalist group, founded in 1974. Over the decade that followed the group used bombings and targeted killings of civilians and police in pursuit of an independent Puerto Rico.[44]

The Weather Underground (the Weathermen) began as a militant faction of the leftist Students for a Democratic Society (SDS) organization, and in 1969 took over the organization. Weathermen leaders inspired by China's Maoists, the Black Panthers and the 1968 student revolts in France, sought to raise awareness of its revolutionary anti-capitalist and anti-Vietnam

[41] Hoffman, p. 16. Aldo, Chaliand, p. 227.
[42] Ibid.
[43] "Backgrounder: The Jewish Defense League", www.adl.org.
[44] Gina M. Perez-Fuerdas Armadas de Liberacion Nacional (FALN), Ency. Of Chicago.

war platform by destroying symbols of government power.[45] In Asia, the Japanese Red Army founded by Fusako Shigenobu in Japan in 1971, attempted to overthrow the Japanese government and start a world revolution. Allied with the Popular Front for the Liberation of Palestine (PFLP), the group committed assassinations, hijacked a commercial Japanese aircraft and sabotaged a Shell oil refinery in Singapore.[46]

Founded in 1976, the Liberation Tigers of Tamil Elam (LTTE or Tamil Tigers) was a militant Tamil nationalist political and paramilitary organization based in Northern Sri Lanka. From its founding by Velupillai Prabhakaran, it waged a secessionist resistance campaign that sought to create an independent Tamil state in the Northern and Eastern regions of Sri Lanka. The conflict originated in measures the majority Sinhalese took that were perceived as attempts to marginalize the Tamil minority. The resistance campaign evolved into the Sri Lankan Civil War, one of the longest armed conflicts in Asia.[47]

In Kenya, because of the ongoing failure of the Kenyan African Union to obtain political reforms from the British through peaceful means, radical activists within the KAU set up a splinter group and organized a more militant kind of nationalism. By 1952, the Mau Mau consisted of Kikuyu fighters, along with some Embu and Meru recruits. The Mau Mau carried out attacks on political opponents, loyalist villages raiding white settlers' farms and destroying livestock.[48] Founded in 1961, Umkhonto we Sizwe (MK) was the military wing of the African National Congress; it waged a guerrilla campaign against the South African apartheid regime and was responsible for many bombings. The South African government subsequently banned the group after classifying it as a terrorist organization. Incidentally, MK's first leader was Nelson

[45] Eric Hobsbawm-Globalisation, Democracy and Terror.

[46] The Japanese Red Army Profile, http://www.start.umd.ed

[47] John Richardson-Paradise Poisoned: Learning About Conflict, Terrorism and Development From Sri Lanka's Civil War, International Centre For Ethnic Studies, 2005, p. 29. Also, Frontline-Sri Lanka: Living With Terror, May, 2002.

[48] How Bennett-Fighting the Mau Mau: The British Army and Counter Insurgency in the Kenya emergency, Cambridge University Press, p. 147.

Mandela, who was tried and imprisoned for the group's act.[49] In the 1980s and 1990s, Islamic militancy in pursuit of religious and political goals increased as many militants drawing inspiration from Iran's 1979 Islamic Revolution. In the 1990s well known violent acts that targeted civilians were the World Trade Centre bombing by Islamic terrorists on February 26, 1993, the Sarin gas attack on the Tokyo Subway by Aum Shinrikyo on March 25, 1995, and the bombing of Okhlahama City's Murrah Federal Building by Timothy Mcveigh, a month later the same year. This period also saw the rise of Single issue terrorism.[50]

Also, during this time, The Red Brigrades, a New Left group was founded by Renato Carcia and Alberto Franceschini in 1970 and based in Italy, sought to create a revolutionary state. The group carried out a series of bombings and kidnappings till the arrests of arrest of Curcio and Franceschini in the mid-1970s.[51]

In the late 20th century in the Americas, the Contras were a counter revolutionary militia formed in 1979 to oppose Nicaragua's Sandinista's government. The Catholic Institution for International Relations asserted in 1987: "The record of the Contras in the field .... is one of consistent and bloody abuse of human rights, murder, torture, mutilation rape arson, destruction and kidnapping.[52]

In the Middle East, between 1982 and 1986, in Lebanon 659 people died in 36 suicide attacks directed against American, French and Israeli forces by 41 individuals having predominantly leftist political beliefs who were adherents of both Christian and Muslim religions. In this context, Hezbollah, ("Party of God") is an Islamist movement and political party officially founded in Lebanon in 1985, then years after the outbreak of that country's civil war. Inspired by Ayatollah Ruhollah Khoemini and the Iranian revolution, the group originally sought an Islamic

[49] Ibid.

[50] "Mcveigh Remorseless About Bombing", Associated Press, March 29, 2001.

[51] "Ed Vulliamy Secret agents, freemasons, fascists...and a top level campaign of political destabilization", The Guardian, December 5, 1990.

[52] "Nicaragua", hrw.org, 27th November, 2015.

revolution in Lebanon and has long fought for the withdrawal of Israeli forces from Lebanon.[53]

Egyptian Islamic Jihad (Al Gamaa Al Islamiyya) is a dedicated Egyptian militant Islamic movement directed dedicated to the establosment of an Islamic state in Egypt. The group was formed in 1980 as an umbrella organization for militant student groups which were formed after the leadership of Muslim Brotherhood renounced violence. It was led by Omar Abdel Raman, who was accused of participation in 1993 World Trade Center bombing. This group was also held responsible for the assassination of Egyptian President Anwar Sadaat. On November 17, 1997, they carried out Luxor Massacre of tourists at the Temple of Hatshepsut, Egypt.[54]

On December 21, 1988, Pan Am Flight 103, a Pan American World Airways Flight from London's Heathrow International Airport New York City's John F. Kennedy International Airport was destroyed mid air over the Scottish town of Lockerbie, killing 270 people including 11 on the ground. On January 31, 2001, Libyan Abdelbaset al-Megrahi was convicted and sentenced to 27 years of imprisonment.[55] The first Palestinian suicide attack took place in 1989 when a member of Palestinian Islamic Jihad ignited a bomb on board Tel Aviv Bus killing 16 people. In the early 1990s, another group, Hamas also became famous for suicide bombings. Sheikh Ahmed Yassin, Abdel Aziz al-Rantissi and Mohammed Taha of the Palestinian wing of Egypt's Muslim Brotherhood had created Hamas in 1987, at the beginning of the first Intifada, an uprising against Israeli rule in Palestinian Territories which mostly consisted of civil disobedience but occasionally escalated into violence. Hamas's militia the Iz ad-Din al-Qasam's Brigades, began it's own suicide bombings against Israel in 1993.[56] Aim Shinrikyo, now known as Aleph, was a Japanese religious group founded by Shoko Asahara in 1984 as a yogic meditation group. Later, in 1990,

[53] Dhar Jamail-"Hezbollah's Transformation", Asia Times, 2007, October.

[54] Lawrence Wright-Loming Tower, Knopf, 2006, p. 123.

[55] BBC News, August 20, 2009.

[56] Mathew Kevitt-Hamas: Politics, Charity and Terrorism In The Service of Jihad, Yale University Press, 2007.

Asahara and 24 other members campaigned for election to the House of Representatives under the banner of Shinrito (Supreme Truth Party). None were voted in and the group began to militarize. Between 1990 and 1995, the group attempted several apparently unsuccessful violent attacks using the methods of biological warfare, using botolin toxin and anthrax spores.[57] In 1985, Air India Flight 182, flying from Canada was blown up by a bomb, while in Irish airspace killing 329 people including 280 Canadian citizens, mostly of Indian birth or descent and 22 Indians. The incident was the deadliest act of air terrorism before 9/11, and the first bombing of a 747 Jumbo Jet setting up a pattern for future air terrorism plot. The crash occurred within hours of the fatal Narita Airport Bombing which also originated from Canada without the passenger for the bag that exploded on the ground. Evidence from the explosion, eye witnesses and wiretaps of the militants pointed to an attempt to actually blow up two airliners simultaneously by members of Babbar Khalsa Khalistan group based in Canada to punish India for attacking the Golden Temple at Amritsar as part of Operation Bluestar launched by the then Prime Minister of India, Mrs. Indira Gandhi to flush out Khalistani terrorists.[58] The Iranian Embassy siege took place in 1980, after a group of six armed men stormed the Iranian Embassy in South Kensington, London. The Government ordered the Special Air Service (SAS), a special force regiment of the British Army to conduct an assault-Operation Nimrod, to rescue the remaining hostages.

This response set the tone for how Western governments would respond to terrorism, replacing an era if negotiation with one of military intervention.[59] Chechen separatists, led by Shamil Basayev, carried out several attacks on Russian targets between 1996 and 2006. In the June, 1995, Budyonnovsk Hospital hostage crisis, Basayev led separatists took over 1, 000 civilian hostage in a hospital in southern interior Russian city of Budyonnovsk. When

[57] CDC Website: Centre For Disease Control And Prevention-Aum Shinrikyo-Once and Future Threat by Kyle B. Olson.

[58] The Statesman, 1984.

[59] McNee, p. 146

Russian Special Forces attempted to free the hostages, 105 civilians and 25 Rusdian troops were killed.[60]

On 23rd October, 2002, 40 to 50 armed Chechens led by Movsar Barayev who claimed allegiance to the Islamist Militant Separatist Movement in Chechnya, seized a crowded Moscow Theatre in Moscow Theater Hostage Crisis. They took 850 hostages demanding the withdrawal of Russian forces from Chechnya and put an end to the Second Chechen War. After two and a half day siege, Russian Spetnaz forces pumped an unknown chemical agent (thought to be fentanyl) into the building's ventilation system and raided it. Roughly 170 people died as a result of this, which drew widespread condemnation from across every corner due to the usage of chemicals.[61]

On September 1, 2004, in Beslan School Hostage Crisis, 32 Chechen separatists led by Basayev took 1300 children and adult hostage at Beslan's School Number One. When Russian authorities did not comply with the rebel demand of withdrawal of Russian troops from Chechnya, 20 adult male hostages were shot. After two days of stalled negotiations, Russian special forces stormed the building. In the ensuing melee 300 died along with 19 Russian Special forces were also killed.[62] The 2004 Madrid Train Bombings (also known as 12-M, 2004) were nearly simultaneous coordinated bombings against the Cercanius commuter train system in Madrid, Spain, - three days before the general election Spain. Two and a half years after the 9/11, in the United States. The explosion killed 191 people and wounded about 1300 people. ETA and al Qaeda were the original suspects as cited by the Spainish government.[63]

The 7th July 2005, London Bombings (Often referred to as 7/7) were a series of coordinated suicide bomb attacks in Central London, which targeted civilians using public transport system

[60] Sebastian Smith-Allah's Mountain: The Battle for Chechnya, Tauris, 2005, p. 200.
[61] The Statesman, 2002.
[62] Ibid, 2004.
[63] CNN, 2005.

during the morning rush hour. 52 civilians were killed and over 700 injured in the attacks. Documents showed that Osama bin laden and Rashid Ruff planned the attacks.[64]

In Norway, 2011, two sequential lone wolf terrorist attacks by right wing extremists Anders Behring Breivik were carried out against the government., the civilians and a workers' youth league (AUF) - run summer camp in Norway, 22nd July, 2011.[65] The attacks claimed a total of 77 lives.[66]

From January 7 to January 9, 2015, a series of five terrorist attacks occurred across the Ile-de-France region particularly in Paris. The attacks killed a total of 17 people in addition to the three perpetrators of the attack and wounding 22 others some of them critically. A fifth shooting attack did not result in any casualty. Al Qaeda in the Arabian peninsula claimed that the attack had been planned years before.[67]

On 7th January, 2015, two Islamist gunmen forced their way into and opened fire in the Paris Headquarters of Charlie Hebdo, shooting and killing tweve and wounding eleven, four of them seriously. On November 13, 2015, three groups of ISIS terrorists performed mass killings in various places of Paris. They killed a total of more than 130 citizens. Hostages were taken in the concert hall "Le Bataclan" for three hours and ninety were killed before special police arrived.[68]

On the morning of 22 March, 2016 three coordinated suicide bombings occurred in Belgium, two at Brussels airport in Zaventem, and one at Maalbeek metro station in Central Brussels. They were referred to as 2016 Brussels attacks. In the attack 32 civilians and three perpetrators were killed and more than 300 people injured. The Islamic State of Iraq and Levant (ISIL) claimed responsibility for the attack.[69]

---

[64] CNN, July 7, 2005.
[65] Ibid.
[66] CNN.com-"Norway honors victims of terrorist attacks."
[67] The Statesman, 2015.
[68] www.telegraph.u.k.com
[69] Kenneth Lasoen-Journal of Strategic Studies, 40(7), 2017, pp. 927–962.

Having discussed the above, the turning point of terrorism came in September, 2011 when a most unassuming but one of the most deadliest figures of world terrorism emerged in the name of Osama bin laden, who ushered in an era of religious fanaticism within terrorism and gave terror a new definition.

Osama bin laden, born in Saudi Arabia in 1957 or 1958, a member of Muslim Brotherhood, was closely advised by Egyptian Islamic Jihad leader Ayman al-Zawahiri, in 1988 founded Al Qaeda (meaning in Arabic "The Base"). It was an Islamic Jihadist movement to replace Western controlled or dominated Muslim countries with Islamic fundamentalist regime. In pursuit of that goal, bin laden issued a 1996 manifesto that vowed violent jihad against US military forces based in Saudi Arabia. On August 7, 1998, individuals associated with Al Qaeda and Egyptian Islamic Jihad carried out simultaneous bombings of two US embassies in Africa killing 224 people. On October, 2012 Al Qaeda carried out the USS Cole bombing, a suicide bombing of the U. S navy destroyer USS Cole, harbored in the Yemeni port of Aden. The bombing killed 17 IS sailors.[70]

On September 11, 2001, nineteen men affiliated with Al Qaeda hijacked four passenger commercial passenger jets all bound for California crashing two of them into the World Trade Center in New York, third into the Pentagon, the Arlington county, Virginia (and the fourth, originally intended to target Washington D.C., either the White House or the US Capital) into an open field near Shanksville, Pennsylvania, after a revolt by the Plane's passengers. As a result of the attacks 2996 people (including 19 hijackers perished and more than 6000 people were injured.[71]

The United States responded by launching the War on Terror. Specifically, on October 7, 2001, it invaded Afghanistan to depose the Taliban which had harbored the Al Qaeda terrorists. Under the Obama administration, the US changed tactics moving away from ground combat with large number of troops, to the use of

[70] CBC News, October 29, 2004.
[71] The Statesman, 2001.

drones and special forces. The campaign eliminated most of the Al Qaeda's senior members, including a strike by Seal Team Six that resulted in the death of Osama bin laden in 2011.[72]

As the Islamic State of Syria and Iraq increased in size and power their attacks were affecting all parts of the world even in their own backyard of Turkey.

On December 27, 2007, two time elected Pakistani Prime Minister Benazir Bhutto was assassinated during a gathering she was having with her supporters. A suicide bomber detonated a bomb along with other extremists against her shooting off guns killing the Prime Minister and 14 other people. She was believed to be the target because she was warning Pakistan along with the world of the uprising Jihadist groups and the extremist groups gaining power. Although Al Qaeda took responsibility for her death; to many Pervez Musharraf was responsible for her death for not taking her concern seriously.

In 2008, India was shaken when more than ten coordinated shooting and bombing attacks took place at six places of the financial capital of India, Mumbai, which was orchestrated by Lashkar-eTaiba a Pakistani Islamic Terrorist Organization with links to the ISI, Pakistan's Secret Service. This has been discussed in the previous chapter.

The attacks which drew widespread condemnation across the world, began on November 26, 2008, and lasted until November 29, 2008, killing at least 173 people and wounding 308.[73] Again, this would remind us of Mumbai Serial Blast in 1993 which for the first time gave us a taste of terror.

On January 14, 2016, a series of terrorist attacks took place Jakarta, Indonesia, resulting in 8 dead. The responsibility of these attacks had been claimed by ISIS. Counter terrorism has named this type of attack as 'Marauding Terrorist Firearms Attack'

---

[72] Ibid., 2011.
[73] The Statesman, 2008.

because of the fast reaction local policemen needed to stop the gunfire attack from the terrorists.[74]

Again, in 2016, the terrorist attack at Holy Artisan Bakery, Dhaka killing and injuring mainly foreigners is wake up sign for us.

This is a warning for the future as ISIS being afraid of losing control in the Middle East may turn to Southeast and South Asia by creating local modules or cells which would act on behalf of the ISIS. This is dangerous as it needs small amount of men to carry out the attacks as it could be done by a lone wolf but the damage they will cause can be devastating. The sign is ominous as recently the way bomb blasts occurred in Bangladesh and Sri Lanka Churches killing hundreds and injuring many. More worrying some is the way children of affluent families are taking up terrorism. So economy may not be the sole reason for growth of terrorism religious fanaticism is also deeply influencing the minds of the young generation.

Again, turning back to India this terrorism which is already a menace in the subcontinent can get triggered off into a holocaust if the dreaded ISIS could link up with the various jihadi groups of India including Kashmir as the latter is already a hot bed of separatist politics marked by anti Indian sentiment. It is to be seen how the Government of India deals with the crisis. Also, we have to see how separatism and terrorism got intertwined in Kashmir.

[74] www.bbcnews.com/world/asia.

6

THE GROWTH OF INSURGENCY IN KASHMIR

The unrest in Jammu and Kashmir, or the Kashmiri Insurgency (also known as Kashmiri Intifada) is a conflict between various Kashmiri separatists and the Government of India. There are some groups that support the complete independence of Kashmir, while others seek Kashmir's accession to Pakistan. The conflict in Jammu and Kashmir has strong Islamist elements among the insurgents with many of the "ultras" identifying with Jihadist movements and supported by such.[1] Thousands of people have died during fighting between the insurgents and the government as well as thousands of civilians who have died as a result of being targeted by the various armed groups.

The Inter Services Intelligence of Pakistan has been accused by India of supporting and training mijahideens to fight on Jammu and Kashmir. In 2015, former President of Pakistan, Pervez Musharraf had admitted that Pakistan had supported and trained insurgent groups in the 1990s.[2] As a result of this, some rights group claimed that since 1989, there have been over 100, 000 deaths and innumerable missing both due to the lure of money offered by

---

[1] Sumantra Bose-Kashmir, Roots of Conflict, Paths To Peace, H. U. P., p. 107.

[2] Business Standard, Press Trust of India, 28th October, 2015.

the Terrorists and the encounter by the security forces.[3] It is to be noted that post independence in 1947-48, at the end of the Ist Indo-Pak War, India controlled most valuable part of Kashmir.[4] While there were sporadic periods of violence there had been no organized insurgency in Kashmir.[5]

During this period, legislative elections were held for the first time in 1951. Sheikh Abdullah, who was an instrumental member on the accession of the state to India, his secular party stood unopposed in the elections more due to the fact of his closeness to Nehru at that time. However, Sheikh Abdullah would fall in and out of the Central Government especially Nehru, and would often to be dismissed, only to be reappointed later. This was when the Sheikh lost his favour with Nehru for his demand of separate Kashmir. This was a time of political instability and power struggle in Jammu and Kashmir.[6] After Sheikh Abdullah's death on 8th September, 1982, his son Farooq Abdullah took over as the Chief Minister of Jammu and Kashmir.

Farooq Abdullah eventually fell out of favour with the Centre as the then Prime Minister of India, Mrs. Indira Gandhi removed him from power with the help of his brother-in-law G. M. Shah. A year later, Abdullah reached an accord with the new Indian Prime Minister Rajiv Gandhi and announced an alliance with the Congress party for the elections of 1987. But the elections were allegedly rigged in favour of Abdullah.[7] Most commentators stated that this led to the beginning of an armed insurgency movement composed in part of those who unfairly lost the elections. Pakistan supplied these groups with logistical support, arms and ammunition, recruits and training.[8]

---

[3] Sumantra Bose-Kashmir, Roots of Conflict, Paths to Peace, H. U. P., p. 107.

[4] Praveen Swami-India, Pakistan and the Secret Jihad, 2006.

[5] Sumantra Bose-Kashmir, Roots of Conflict and Paths to Peace, HUP, pp. 107–109.

[6] Mohd. Abbas Wani-"Beg. of Terrorism in J & K, Indian Stream Research Journal, 2014.

[7] "Kashmir in Insurgency", BBC News, 22nd February, 2017.

[8] Arif Jamar-The Untold Story of Jihad in Kashmir, 2009.

In the second half of 1989, the alleged assassinations of Indians by Jammu and Kashmir Liberation Front (JKLF) was intensified. Over the months more than a hundred officials were killed to paralyze government's administrative and intelligence apparatus. The daughter of the then interior minister, Mufti Mohammed Syed, was kidnapped in December and four terrorists had to be released in return for her freedom. This event led to mass celebration all over the valley. Farooq Abdullah resigned in January after the appointment of Jamohan Malhotra as the Governor of Jammu and Kashmir. Subsequently, the state was placed under Governor's Rule on the basis of Article 92 of state constitution.[9] It is to be mentioned here the main operators of politics in Kashmir, which are the following:

1. Harkat-ul-Jihad-al-Islami;
2. Lashkar-eTaiba;
3. Jaish-e-Mohammed;
4. Hizbul Mujahedeen
5. Harkat-ul-Mujahideen;
6. Al Badr;
7. Jammu and Kashmir Liberation Front; and
8. ISIL-KP. They are supported by Pakistan, Taliban and Al Qaeda.[10]

Under JKLF's leadership, on January 21–23, 1989, large scale protests were organized in the valley. In response to this largely explosive situation, paramilitary units of BSF and CRPF were called. These units were called in by the Government to combat Maoist and Northeastern insurgency. The challenge to them in this situation was not posed by armed insurgents but by the stone pelters. Now, the underground militant movement was transformed into a mass movement. To curb the situation, Armed Forces Special Power Act (AFSA) was imposed on Kashmir in September, 1990 to suppress the insurgency by giving armed forces

---

[9] Navnita Chadha Behera-Kashmir Demystified, Washington D.C., 2006, Brookings Inst. Press.

[10] The New York Times, 21st January, 2007, an Article by Carlotta Galli.

the powers to kill and arrest without warrant to maintain public order. During this time, the dominant tactic involved killing of a prominent figure in public gathering to push forces in action and the public prevented them from capturing these insurgents. These sprouting of sympathisers in Kashmir forced the Indian army to lose their patience and adopt hardline approach.[11]

With JKLF at the forefront, large number of militant groups like Allah Tigers, Peopl's League and Hizb-i-Islamia had sprung up. Weapons were smuggled on a large scale from Pakistan. In Kashmir the JKLF was led by Ashfaq Majid Wani, Yasin Bhat, Hamid Sheikh Yasin Malik, and Javed Mir. To counter this growing pro-Pakistani sentiment in Kashmir, Indian media associated it exclusively with Pakistan. The JKLF distinctly used Islamic themes to mobilize crowd and justify violence. They sought to establish an Islamic Democratic State where the rights of minorities would be protected according to Quran and Sunna and economy would be organized on the principles of Islamic socialism.[12]

During the early period of militancy in Kashmir in 1989, multiple militant groups strove to Islamise Kashmiri culture and political set up to create a conducive environment for the merger of Kashmir with Pakistan. Numerous Islamist groups were formed in the early 1990s which emerged advocating Nizam-e-Mustafa (Rule of Mohammed) as the objective of their struggle. Militant groups like Hizbul Mujahedeen Jamaat-e-Islami asserted that the struggle of Kashmir would continue till Islamic Caliphate was achieved. Murder of Kashmiri Hindus, intellectuals, liberals and activists were described necessarily to get rid of unislamic elements.[13] At one point of time, concurrently all cinema houses, beauty parlors, wine shops, bars, video parlors, use of cosmetics and similar things were banned by militant groups. Many militant

[11] Navnita Chadha Behera- Kashmir Demystified, Washington D.C., Brookings Inst. Press.

[12] Sumantra Bose-Kashmir Roots of Conflict, Paths To Peace, 2003, Cambridge, Harvard University Press, p. 146.

[13] M. G. Chitkara-Kashmir; LOC, A. P. H. Publishing, p. 123.

organizations like Al Baqr, People's League, Wahdat-e-Islam, and Allah Tigers imposed restrictions like banning cigarettes, restrictions on Kashmiri girls etc.[14] Apart from militancy, Kashmir was witnessing Islamization during 1980s when Abdullah government changed the names of about 2500 villages from their native names to new Islamic names. Sheikh Abdullah also started delivering communal speeches in mosques similar to his speeches in the 1930s. Additionally, he referred Kashmiri Pandits as "mukhbir" or informers of the Indian government.[15]

Beginning in 2004, Pakistan began to end its support for insurgents in Kashmir. This happened because terrorist groups linked to Kashmir twice tried to assassinate

Pakistani President General Pervez Musharraf. His successor Asif Ali Zardari also continued the policy, calling insurgents in Kashmir "terrorists".[16] Although, it is unclear if Pakistan's Intelligence Agency, the Inter Services Intelligence (ISI) thought to be the one who were aiding and controlling the insurgency in Kashmir was following Pakistani Government's commitment to end support to the insurgents in Kashmir.[17]

It is noteworthy that in the early 2000, after the Kargil War President General Pervez Musharraf was really contemplating a permanent solution to the Kashmir problem for which he met the Indian Prime Minister Atal Behari Vajpayee in 2001, at the Agra Summit. Again, it was well known that the family of Benazir Bhutto was slightly lenient towards India. All these developments were not to the Vikings of the ISI *vis-a-vis* the terrorists who were now instigated by the ISI to cause disturbances in Kashmir and to kill any one who wanted to solve Kashmir problem. This showed that terrorism has no country, no ideology only motivated by self interests. Although the Hoky Quran talks of peaceful coexistence the terrorists never cared for that; they used religion to their liking

---

[14] Richard L. Benkin-What is moderate Islam?, Lexington Books, p. 47.

[15] "Kashmir Violence-Possible Solution", The Shillong Times, 24th February, 2019.

[16] Bret Stevens-"The Most Difficult Job In The World.", 4th Oct., 2008, The Wall St. Jour.

[17] Ibid.

for meeting their interests only. The ISI of Pakistan fostered the terrorists to always destabilize India. They do not want solution much to the ignorance of the Government otherwise their income from narcotics smuggling and their intention of always using Kashmir as a political card both at domestic and international levels would be lost. In Pakistan, the Government is a pawn at the hands of the ISI and military. Even if the Government shows good intention, it will be thwarted and ultimately the Government might be dislodged and replaced by a military government.[18]

Following the growth of Islamisation in the Kashmir valley, during the 1987 state elections, various Islamic anti-establishment groups like Jamaat-e-Islami Kashmir were organized under a single banner, named Muslim United Front (MUF) that is largely current Hurriyat. M.U.F.'s election manifesto stressed the need for a solution to all outstanding issues according to Shimla Agreement, work for Islamic unity and against political interference from the centre. Their slogan was wanting the law of Quran in the Assembly. But the MUF won only four seats though it secured 31% of the votes in the Asseembly. However, the elections were widely believed to have been rigged, changing the course of politics. The insurgency was sparked off by the apparent rigging of state elections in 1987. The Pakistani Inter Services Intelligence has encouraged and aided the Kashmir Independence Movement through insurgency due to its dispute regarding legitimacy of Indian rule in Kashmir, as the insurgency was an easy way to keep Indian troops distracted and cause international condemnation of India.[19]

Having discussed the main actors playing their roles in Kashmir, let us see how insurgency crept in the Kashmir valley. It is said that after the invasion of Afghanistan by Soviat Union, Mujahedeen fighters with the aid of Pakistan, slowly infiltrated Kashmir with the goal of spreading radical Islamist Ideology.[20]

---

[18] Ibid.

[19] Ibid.

[20] BBC News-"Kashmir Insurgency", 21 February, 2017.

It is to be remembered that Jammu and Kashmir is the only Muslim majority state in a Hindu majority country. Indian-American journalist Asra Nomani stated that while India itself was a secular state when compared to Hindus as a whole, Muslims are found to be politically, culturally and economically marginalized.[21]

Again, the government's decision to transfer 99 acres of forest land near Amarnath to the Amarnath Shrine Board for setting up temporary shelters and facilities for the Hindu pilgrims solidified this feeling and led to one of the largest protest rallies in Jammu and Kashmir. It must be mentioned here that the cave of Amarnath was discovered by a Muslim peasant while he went there to graze his sheep and he and his successors are one of the chief beneficiaries of the Amarnath collections.[22]

After insurgency started in the Kashmir valley due to the above factors in the late 1980s, Indian troops entered Kashmir valley to control the situation. Some analysts have suggested that the number of Indian troops in Jammu and Kashmir was close to around 600,000 although estimates vary and the Indian government refuses to release actual figures of troops in the region. The troops have been accused and held accountable for several humanitarian abuses and have engaged in mass extrajudicial killings, torture, rape and sexual abuse.[23]

Indian security forces have been implicated in many reports for enforced disappearances of thousands of Kashmiris though the Indian security forces deny this. Human Rights Activists estimated that the number of disappeared to 8000, last seen in government detention. The disappeared are believed to be dumped in thousands of mass graves across Kashmir. A State Human rights Commission enquiry in 2011 has confirmed there were thousands

---

21 Asra Q Nomani-"Muslims: India's New Untouchables", Los Angels Times, Dec. 1, 2008.

22 Jyoti Thottam-"Valley in Tears", The Time Magazine, 4th September, 2008.

23 Asad Hashim-Timeline: India Pakistan Relations, 27 May, 2014, AlJazeera Newspaper.

of bullet-ridden bodies buried in unmarked graves across Jammu and Kashmir. Of the 2730 bodies uncovered in 4 out of 14 districts, 574 bodies were identified as locals in contrast to the Indian government insistence that all the graves belonged to the foreign militants.[24]

However, the army deny the accusations. Ex Army Chief General V. K. Singh on 24 October, 2010 reported that 104 Army personnel had been punished in Jammu and Kashmir including 39 officers in this regard. He also said that 95% of the allegations of human rights abuses against Indian Army have proved to be false. He further remarked that these allegations were made with an ulterior motive to malign the army.[25] But according to Human Rights Watch, the military courts in India in general are not competent enough to deal with the serious cases of human rights abuses and are responsible for covering up evidence and protecting the involved officers. Amnesty International in a report of 2015 made similar allegations regarding impartiality and independence of the army authorities dealing with human rights violations.[26]

Military personnel in J & K, operate under impunity and emergency powers granted to them by the Central Government. These powers allowed the military to curtail civil liberty and thus creating further support for insurgency. The insurgents have also abused human rights engaging in what some thought an ethnic cleansing by exterminating Kashmiri Pandits from the valley of Kashmir. The government's inability to protect the people both from its own troops and the insurgency had further eroded support for the govt.[27] Amnesty International accused the security forces of exploiting the Armed Forces Special Powers Act (AFSPA) that enable them to hold prisoners without any trial. The Army sources maintained that any move to revoke the AFSPA in Jammu and Kashmir, would be detrimental to the security of the valley.and would provide a boost for the terrorists. However, these human

---

[24] Lydia Polgreen-Mass Graves Hold Thousands: New York Times, 22 August, 2011.
[25] Daily News And Analysis, 24 October, 2010.
[26] Reader, Correspondent, Kashmir Reader, 3rd September, 2016.
[27] www.hrg.org.

rights violations are said to have contributed to the rise of resistance in Kashmir.[28]

Psychologist Waheeda Khan explaining the rebellious nature of the Kashmiris, said that because of the tense situation in the valley from 1990s, the generation gap between the parents and young children has increased. Young generations tend to blame their parents for failing to do anything about the political situation. So they start experimenting with their own aggressive ways to show their curved feelings and would go against any authority.

A prominent psychiatrist of the valley, Margoob described that children and teenagers are much more vulnerable to passionate actions and reactions, since the young minds are yet to completely develop psychological mechanisms. When they assume they are pushed against the wall, emotions take over their senses without thinking of the consequences. This explains the reason of increasing number of girl student protesters in Kashmir valley, actively participating in anti government demonstrations which was unprecedented. Also, young people could easily identify themselves with groups rather than with their individual identities. It leads to psychological distress which causes anti social behavior and aggressive attitude. Often this situation gets worsened with the availability of weapons and people becoming familiar to violence after being exposed to conflict for such a long time.

Waheeda Khan further remarked that the major concern for this generation of children who have been exposed to violence for such a long period, in the long run, when they would reach adulthood, might think violence was the only fair means of solving ethnic, religious or political differences in their lives.[29]

[28] Malini Parthasarathy- "Understanding Kashmir's Stone Pelters", The Hindu, 24 May, 2017. (Today's protesters might shout anti-India slogans such as azaadi, but their anger is specifically directed at the security forces in the context of brutal killings of innocent boys..."

[29] Waheeda Khan-Conflict in Kashmir, 2015, pp. 90–91.

From the time of 2008 protests and 2010 unrest, the turmoil in the Kashmir valley has taken a new dimension when people, particularly youngsters of the Kashmir valley have started pelting stones on security forces to express their aggression and protest for the loss of freedom. In turn, they get attacked by the armed personnel with pellets, rubber bullets, sling shots and tear gas shells. This leads to eye and several other kinds of injuries to many people. Security forces also face injuries, and sometimes get beaten up during these events. According to Waheeda Khan, most of the 'stone pelters' are school and college going students. Large number of them get arrested during these events for allegedly resorting to stone pelting. According to political activist Mannan Bukhari, Kashmiris made stone, an easily accessible and defenceless weapon, their weapon of choice for protest.[30]

Even, the Islamic separatist militants are accused of violence against Kashmir populace. They commit serious human rights violations like summary execution, rape and torture. The militants have kidnapped and killed many civil servants and suspected informers. Human Rights Watch alleged that thousands of civilian Kashmiri Hindus have been killed over the past ten years by Islamic Militant Organizations or Muslim mobs. The militants committed war rape during the 1980s. Tens of thousands of Kashmiri Pandits have emigrated as a result of the violence. Estimates of the displaced varies from 170000 to 700000. Thousands of Kashmiri Pandits had to move to Jammu because of militancy.[31]

In the context of the above, let us discuss the sequence of events that took place since 1989. In July and August, 1989, three CRPF personnel and a politician Mohd. Yusuf Halwai if NC/F were killed.[32];

[30] Waheeda Khan-Conflict In Kashmir, 2015, pp. 90–91. Also, Mannan Bukhari, Kashmir, Scars of Pellet Gun, The Brutal Face of Suppression, Patridge Publishing, p. 44.

[31] Kanchan Gupta (19th January, 2005)- "19.1.90.: When Kashmiri Pandits Fled Islamic Terror", Rediff.com.

[32] "Chronicle of Important events/dates in J & K's political history.", Jammu-Kashmir.com, 14th June, 2015.

In 1989, Rubaiya Sayeed, daughter of Mufti Mohammed Sayeed, was kidnapped;

In 1995, kidnapping of western tourists in Jammu and Kashmir-six foreign trekkers were kidnapped Al Faran from Anantnag district. One was beheaded later, one escaped and the other four remained missing, presumably killed;

In 1997, Sangrampora Massacre took place on 22nd March, 1997 when seven Kashmiri Pandits were killed in Sangrampore village in Budgaon district;

In 1998, in January 1998, 24 Kashmiri Pandits living in the village of Wandhama, were massacred by Pakistani militants. According to the testimony of one of the survivors, the militants dressed themselves up as officers of the Indian army, entered their houses and started firing blindly. This incident was significant because it coincided with former US President Bill Clinton's visit to India and New Delhi highlighted the massacre to prove Pakistan supported terrorism Kashmir.[33]

In 1998, what was known as Prankote Massacre, 26 Hindu villagers of Udhampur were killed by the militants. In the same year, 25 Hindu villagers killed on 19th June, 1998, by Islamic militants.

In 2000, 30 Hindu Amarnath pilgrims were massacred by the militants. In the same year 36 Sikhs were massacred by LET in what was known as Chittisinghpura Massacre.

In 2001, 1st October, the terrorists bombed the Jammu and Kashmir Legislative Assembly in Srinagar killing 38.

In 2002, the first attack on Raghunath Temple occurred on 30th March, 2002 when two suicide bombers attacked the temple. Eleven persons including three security forces personnel were killed and twenty were injured. The fidayen suicide squad attacked the Temple a second time on 24 November, 2002, when two suicide

[33] Wandhama Massacre Report, 9th October, 1999.

bombers stormed the temple and killed 14 devotees and injured 45 others.

On 13th July, 2002, armed militants believed to be a part of Lashkar-eTaiba threw hand grenades at the Qasim Nagar Market in Srinagar, known as Qasim Nagar Massacre and then fired on civilians standing nearby killing 27 and injuring many more.

On 23rd March, 2003, 24 Hindus were killed in Nandimarg, Kashmir by Lashkar-eTaiba militants.

On 20th July, 2005, a car bomb exploded near an Indian army armoured vehicle in the famous Church Lane area in Srinagar killing 4 Indian army personnel, one civilian and a suicide bomber. Militant group Hizbul Mujahedeen claimed responsibility for the attack. Again, on 29th July, 2005, a militant attacked Srinagar"s City Center at Budshah Chowk killing 2 and injuring more than 17 people, who were mostly journalists. Further, on with October, 2005, suspected Kashmiri militants killed Jammu and Kashmir's then education minister Abdul Ghani Lone, a prominent All Party Hurriyat Conference Leader. Militant group called Al Mansurin claimed responsibility for the attack. Unidentified gunmen killed him during a memorial rally at Srinagar. The assassination resulted in a widespread demonstration against the Indian Security Forces for failing to provide enough security cover for Lone.[34]

On 3rd May, 2006, militants massacred 35 Hindus in Doda and Udhampur districts of Jammu and Kashmir.[35] Again, on 12th June, 2006, one person was killed and 31 were wounded when terrorists hurled three hand grenades on Vaishnodevi Shrine-bound bus at the general bus stand.[36]

After a lull in insurgency in Kashmir valley for quite a few years, the terrorists struck again when on 5th December, 2014, the year when there was a change of administration at the Centre, four

[34] Human Rights Watch World Report, 2005.
[35] Tribune News Services, 4th May, 2006.
[36] S. P. Sharma- "Terror in Jammu, Anantnag," The Tribune, 13 June, 2006.

attacks were made on army, police and civilians resulting in 21 deaths and several injured. Their motive was to disrupt the ongoing Assembly elections.[37]

On 2nd January, 2016, six to seven terrorists heavily armed and dressed in army fatigues attacked the Indian Air Force Base at Pathankot in the early morning after hijacking a police jeep a night before and broke through the parameter fence. The attack was sudden resulting in the death of seven security personnel and wounding twenty five others. Despite Intelligence input of an impending attack on the eve of Republic Day, no proper safeguards were taken.[38]

Again, on 18th September, 2016, four heavily armed men swooped on the army base camp around 5 a.m. at Uri during shift changing catching everybody by surprise which resulted in the death of 19 personnel and injuring 30. Though the four perpetrators of the attack were killed but a question mark was raised about the safeguard of our security personnel despite having state of the art warning equipments and early intelligence inputs. India suspected that members of Lashkar-eTaiba and Jaish-e-Mohammed sponsored by Masood Azar were behind these attacks. As a response, India destroyed the terror launchpad at Muzaffarbad in the first surgical strike nearly ten days after Uri attack.[39]

Two years later, i.e. on 10th February, 2018, Jaissh-e-Mohammed Terrorists attacked Sunjuwan army camp in Jammu and Kashmir. As a result of this, six Indian soldiers, four terrorists, and one civilian died and eleven others were wounded.[40]

Perhaps the last nail on the coffin had been put when on 14th February, 2019 Pulwama attack took place, whereby an explosive laden car driven by believed to be Jaish-e-Mohammed terrorist rammed into an army convoy preparing to depart killing 46

[37] December 5, 2014, The Hindu.
[38] The Statesman, January, 2016.
[39] Ibid.
[40] The Statesman, February, 2018.

soldiers and wounding 20. In this case as before Intelligence warning was there but the security personnel were left to defend themselves. It is very surprising how the car broke into the convoy when it is to be guarded. Also despite having modern radars and warning systems no precaution was taken to protect the army. India's response was surgical strike 2 as the Indian strike aircrafts crossed deep into Pakistan and supposedly destroyed the terrorist training camps run by Masood Azhar in the early morning of 26th February, 2019.[41]

According to the army data, quoted by Reuters, at least 70 young Kashmiris joined the insurgency in 2014. As per army records, most have joined the banned militant group Lashkar-eTaiba, which was accused of carrying out attacks on the city of Mumbai in 2008. Two of the new recruits are doctorates and eight were post graduates.[42] According to BBC that despite a Pakistani ban on militant activities in 2006, its fighters continued to attempt infiltrations into Indian administered Kashmir. These attempts were curtailed, however, when people living along the Line of Control started to hold public protest against the activities of the insurgent groups.[43]

Since 2014, there is a change of tactics on pat of the militants as they now have targeted security forces instead of general public. This was in order to regain the confidence of the people as the security forces are hated both by the public as well as the trrorists. The attack on general targets have isolated the terrorists. So there was a change of strategy. Whatever, the targets of the different militant groups, survey made in 2010 of the general Kashmiris found that 43% of Jammu and Kashmir and 44% of the Pak Occupied Kashmir wanted independence both from India and Pakistan as was visualized by Sheikh Abdullah, with support for independence movement unevenly distributed across the region, while only 2% of the people want to join with Pakistan. (As per data provided by The Times of India.)

---

[41] The Statesman, February, 2019
[42] The Express Tribune, 25 June, 2015
[43] BBC News.com

To be noted that over the last two years the militants groups like Lashkar-eTaiba has split into two factions: Al Mandurin and Al Nasirin. Another new group had emerged in the form of "Save Kashmir Movement." Harkat-ul-Mujahideen, formerly known as Harkat-ul-Ansar, and Lashkar-eTaiba are believed to be operating from Muzaffarabad, Azad Kashmir and Muridke all in Pak Occupied Kashmir.

It is unclear whether if Al Qaeda has made his base in POK Jammu and Kashmir. Donald Rumsfeld suggested that Al Qaeda is operating from POK but there is no ground evidence. Even, the ISIS, whose base is destroyed at Syria have not been able to make an impact on this part of the subcontinent so far.[44]

According to Sumantra Bose-Kashmir: Roots of Conflict, Paths To Peace, around 40000 to 80000 people died including civilians, security forces and militants from 1989 to 2002 throughout Jammu and Kashmir. More than 5000 personnel, 14000 people, and 15937 militants including 3000 from outside. Also till date there has been 58000 incidents of violence are reported. In counter insurgency operations 40000 firearms, 160000 explosive devices and over 6 million rounds of assorted ammunition have been captured. As per data provided by J & K Coalition of Civil Society over 80000 people have been killed by the security forces.

Having discussed the rise of insurgency in Kashmir, we have to look into the fact of countering the menace of terrorism which is now a world wide phenomenon.

[44] The Times of India.

7

KASHMIR - WHERE DO WE GO?

Kashmir is alive political issue in India in a way it has never been before. The India of 1990s had to deal with an insurgency and managed without worrying about national machismo. This is no longer the case.[1] National Conference President and veteran leader Farooq Abdullah once commented that situation in Kashmir was alarming. But cautioned that the future of Kashmiris did not lie with Pakistan. People of Kashmir were intoxicated by Azadi. He said, "People of Kashmir cannot go to the country they were dreaming of and that Pakistan was not the future for Kashmiris. Don't mislead the people towards destruction." Referring to the situation in Kashmir, Abdullah further said, "Situation in Kashmir is alarming. If the situation remains so, people at all places will sacrifice their lives for martyrdom.

"If we have to come out of this storm, then it is must to resolve Kashmir issue as early as possible.... The young people of Kashmir are seeing their future dark. To improve the future of the boys, the government has to see it that constitution is followed in letter and spirit." Suggesting that everyone take the responsibility for the situation Kashmiri youth were caught, Abdullah said, "We created the situation we are seeing our youth in trouble. Urging

---

[1] Mihir Swarup Sharma-Kashmir's Troubled Future, www.orfonline.org.

the state to be self reliant, and calling for greater autonomy, Abdullah said, "Autonomy has to be restored for the honour of the people and the state."[2]

In the Valley's history, there are several points that could be made about what it implies for the future. None of them are anything but deeply disturbing. The first is that there has been a steady increase in violence in the valley since 2014. This has multiple reasons, but the fact that New Delhi has squandered the gains from the ten years of relative quiet prior to 2014 is perhaps the biggest. Rather than trying to integrate more Kashmiris into the mainstream in the years since then the central govt has turned Kashmir into a political issue that it wishes to use to win votes in the Hindi heartland.[3]

The valley was no paradise prior to 2014, but the escalation of violence since 2014 is starkly visible. The number of terrorist incidents, according to Union Home Ministry's numbers that were presented to the Parliament has risen steadily - from 222 in 2014 to 614 in 2018. Te number of security force personnel killed has similarly shot up from 47 in 2014 to 80 in 2017 and 91 in 2018.[4]

When the current government came into power, it abandoned the long standing ceasefire protocol on the Line of Control. This was made to combat infiltrations. But the real problem cropped up as local young people were now taking up guns like the 1990s. Rather than worrying about foreign militants, we should have been concerned about the radicalization of the locals like the 20 year old who drove the Pulwama car bomb. The return of home grown militancy is the second point.[5] While the low level brutality of an intrusive police state through the 2000s and 2010s - which used detention and checkpoints as a matter of course was enough to ensure that an entire generation of Kashmiris has been lost to the

---

[2] The New Indian Express, 4th April, 2018.

[3] Mihir Swarup Sharma-Kashmir's Troubled Future, in Business Standard, www.orfonline.org.

[4] Ibid.

[5] Mihir Swarup Sharna, Business Standard, www.orfonline.org.

Indian state. This is a fact that there has been a communication gap between the locals and the centre. For when in 1999, Kargil War occurred it was the local Gujjars who informed the security forces of the identity of the intruders. But since 2014, be it Pathankot, Uri or Pulwama there was no such information coming from the locals before hand. Moreover, it was the locals who supported with supplies to the terrorists.[6]

The third worry is the changing nature of the Islamists' tactics. Tactics can easily be copied from insurgents and terrorists across the world. Intelligence about this attack came in as a 'Syria-style car bomb.' Kashmir has seen few suicide attacks - in fact the Jaish-e-Mohammed pioneered them in an attack on Srinagar"s Badami Bagh cantonment in 2000. A valley full of IEDs, car bombs and suicide bombers is a different proposition from what security forces have had to face before.[7]

Fourthly, the strategy of the militants have also changed. The Jihadists have sought to target military or police specifically. Partly as a consequence, more civilians are sympathetic to the militants than in the 1990s. Combined with increasing religious radicalization - the replacement of local religious traditions with harder, more nihilistic imports from the Middle East - this means that the army and the paramilitary forces have a far harder job. They have already complained about civilian crowd forming to protect areas where the militants are reportedly holed up. Fighting terrorists is one thing. Fighting insurgents is worse. Fighting a population is worst of all.[8]

Fifthly, the impact of neighborhood development can clearly be felt. The United State's promise of a precipitate withdrawal from Afghanistan is dangerous. Not only it will inspire Jihadists everywhere the same way that the U.S.S.R.s' defeat by the Mujahedeen did, the confidence of the Pakistani military establishment given this unexpected departure and the solid

---

[6] Ibid.
[7] Ibid.
[8] Ibid

support of Beijing has soared. The last time Pakistan backed jihadists were at a loose end after superpower withdrawal, three decades ago, the valley exploded. We should deeply fear the consequences of an easing of pressure on Pakistan's western border.[9]

Adding to this challenge, the well springs of the latest surge in violence in Kashmir are not limited to the regional dispute between India and Pakistan. A new generation of Kashmiri firebrands is finding its voice. India has not found a way to respond to the generation's particular capacity for popular mobilization and ruthless intimidation.[10]

Another point is the Kashmir dispute has become increasingly layered and fragmented with territorial, legal and political dimensions. One obstacle in attempt to solve the Kashmir Conundrum has been a lack of Agreement between the two countries on the definition of the problem. Pakistan's claim to Kashmir is based on religion while India's based upon its ruler accession to it in 1947. Neither countries have tried to ascertain what the Kashmiris want. Kashmiri aspirations stem from one little understood consequence of the partition of British India. In 1947, when India and Pakistan gained their freedom the Kashmiris lost theirs. They lost the freedom to live, travel, study and do business in any part of the subcontinent. And they got nothing in return. Both India and Pakistan gave their parts of Kashmir autonomy bordering on independence in theory but denied them even a semblance of democratic freedom in practice. Kashmiris therefore felt doubly betrayed. This feeling is shared by the Kashmiris on both sides of the Line of Control. Their demand for freedom is therefore is not so much a demand for separation from the two countries as a demand for the restoration of their lost freedom and their democratic rights they were promised but never wholly given.[11]

---

[9] Mihir Swarup Sharma-Business Standard, www.onfonline.org.

[10] Council on Foreign Relations, Solving The Kashmir Conundrum, 24 October, 2010.

[11] Ibid.

There is also a contemporary dimension to Kashmir: the stirrings of a national self determination movement among Kashmiri Muslims. Encouraged by neither India nor Pakistan, it burst into full view in late 1989, and threatens the integrity of both states. There are two or three new generations of valley Muslims, educated and trained in India but with a window open to a wider world. Angry and resentful at their treatment by New Delhi and not attracted to even a democratic Pakistan, they look to Afghanistan, Iran, the Middle East and Eastern Europe for models and to emigre in America, Britain and Canada for material support. Further, in an era when the international economy is fast changing (including the advent of self-sustaining "tourist destinations") and the prospect of direct linkage of Central Asia and Kashmir, the old argument that Kashmir is not eco. self sufficient unless it is attached to a major state has lost credibility.[12]

There is a Punjabi saying that "three things are improved by beating: women, wheat and a jat." The quotes are representative of a wider view to the extent that many Pakistanis believe that India only responds to pressure and that many Indians deny that Pakistan has any legitimate role Kashmir except to end its support of the militants. Kashmiris themselves both Hindus and Muslims have now tasted violence of a sort never experienced before as they undergo a terrible ordeal.[13]

After 1971 Kashmir ceased to be the cause of bad India-Pakistan relations but it remains a cause. It is a symbol of their inability to compose their differences and live in peace. Kashmir is thus both cause and effect, which makes it so difficult to conceptualize as a political issue. Again, there is a sense of suspicion among the Kashmiris - while the valley Muslims felt aggrieved that they they are dominated by outsiders from India proper, other Kashmiri groups, especially the valley Hindus and the largely Buddhist population of Ladakh, fear the dominance of the state by the valley Muslims. Thus, a number of proposals have suggested the

[12] Stephen P. Cohen: Kashmir: The Road Ahead, www.brookings.edu, March, 1995.
[13] Stephen P. Cohen-Kashmir: Roads Ahead, www.brookings.edu.

possibility of separating the valley from other regions (Azad Kashmir, Ladakh, Jammu), and allocating parts of Jammu and Kashmir to India and Pakistan, leaving to the end the intensely disputed Valley. Here the appropriate analogy is the Middle East Peace Process, where the overall strategy is to leave to the end such very contentious issues as the status of Jerusalem.[14]

Second, there are, outside the propaganda mills of Delhi and Islamabad, remarkably diverse views on Kashmir both in India and Pakistan. Kashmir is not viewed in the same light by all Indians and Pakstanis. Any one who travelled throughout South Asia during the height of the 1990 Kashmir crisis quickly became aware that the further one was from Delhi and Islamabad the less passion there was about Kashmir. In Madras, Kolkata, Hyderabad (Deccan) and Bombay, Kashmir is seen as New Delhi's obsession; in Karachi, Quetta, Peshawar and Hyderabad (Sindh) it is seen as a secondary issue, relations with Islamabad and the Punjab come first. Indeed the size of demonstrations on behalf of the Kashmiri revolution in all Pakistani cities are in direct proportion to the presence of large Kashmiri populations. "Kashmir" is neither a homogeneous issue within the states of Azad Kashmir and Jammu and Kashmir nor within India and Pakistan. It is to be mentioned that bilateral diplomacy having collapsed between India and Pakistan, there has been, over the past year, a number of incidents in which the diplomats of both sides have been harassed, and even beaten, by security forces, and the intelligence services of both countries have harassed ordinary scholars and journalists attending functions in each other's country. Recent reports indicate that some in Pakistan now see some value in perpetuating the crisis over Siachen, while being "soft" on offers to open up nuclear facilities for inspection, as part of a complex game of getting outsiders, especially, the United States to come down harder still with Delhi. These verbal games are brilliantly played by both sides, but also reveal a lack of interest in achieving a settlement.[15]

---

[14] Ibid.

[15] Stephen P Cohen-Kashmir: The Road Ahead

Third, it is important to recognize the crucial role of time, and timing, in resolving the Kashmir problem. Ironically, one of the obstacles to reaching a solution is the belief, on all sides of the dispute that "time is on our side". Since the Kashmir problem has been mismanaged by two generations of Indians and Pakstanis (and Kashmiris must accept responsibility also, for their own errors of omission and commission), there is no age group, except perhaps amongst new generation of South Asians, who believe that the time has come for a solution. And timing is crucial.[16]

We don't know what steps should be taken first and what should be the last one, but like proposals to resolve 'Arab-Israeli dispute', "solutions" to Kashmir problem must operate at many levels. This suggests both caution and flexibility. But it doesn't suggest that doing nothing is the best choice. The examples of the Middle East, South Africa, and perhaps of Ireland, indicate that seemingly intractable disputes can be resolved or ameliorated, by patience, outside encouragement and above all, a strategy that will address the many dimensions of these complex problems.[17]

Not too many years ago, Indians and Pakstanis took a disparaging view of these other conflicts, and argued that they were successfully managing South Asia. Now their region stands out as conflict ridden, nuclear prone and on the edge of war.[18] The only solution that should be ruled out is doing nothing. Time will not heal the Kashmir problem. Time has made things worse for Kashmir. If a strategy for resolution of this conflict had begun in the early or mid-1980s then we would have averted some of the crises that arose later in that decade and certainly would not have regarded Kashmir now as one of the world's nuclear flashpoints. To those who would argue that the situation was not ripe for a solution it should be pointed out that not only are one hundred million Indian Muslims held hostage by the fate of Kashmir but in reality a billion people are held hostage by the dispute itself. Imagine what South Asia would be if India and Pakistan were to

[16] Ibid.
[17] Ibid.
[18] Stephen P Cohen-Kashmir: The Road Ahead, March 1, 1995, www.brookings.edu.

cooperate not only on bilateral trade, water and population issues but on preserving the strategic unity of South Asia. Each would then be truly counted among the great regional powers.[19]

Having discussed the above, we have to first ask what ails Kashmir and its people? Leaving apart the socio-eco-pol.-religious questions which have always hurt the Kashmiris, we have to look into the psyche of the people there, esp. today's generation. We have to make them believe that they are capable of doing great things and not get involved in petty matters. We have to make the world as well as ourselves convince that Kashmir and Kashmiris are not aliens, they are us and of this world. We have to give back the generation of today esp. in Kashmir their identity which they are losing by being aggressive and getting secessionist. We have to first make a difference between insurgents and terrorists. Insurgency is a temporary phenomenon but terrorism is a deep seeded thing where religion is deeply rooted that gives rise to religious fanaticism. Another incident which is alarming is that not all the new comers to insurgency are from economically deprived classes but from affluent families. We have to segregate them and other young insurgents of today, counsel them give them opportunities at a subsidized rate, pick the best of the lot, groom them and give them the scope for higher studies and give them the window to go to a better world. Religious fanaticism is deep seeded in them and so they will need better counseling. We have to increase mass contacts and isolate the terrorists. We have to make them realise what terrorists are doing are being guided by narrow ideas and have no ideology only narrow interests. This counseling is a long drawn process but in the long run will benefit the society.

[19] Ibid.

8

PROBABLE SOLUTIONS

Most Kashmiris want independence from both India and Pakistan whether openly or secretly even if they don't admit this to the media. This is the third, though not workable solution of a Kashmiri plebiscite under United Nations Security Council Resolution 47 which requires Pakistan to first withdraw her troops from Kashmir. India would also not give her consent for this because it would be politically unacceptable in the country and Kashmir hates both India and Pakistan because of the loss of their basic freedom as human beings. Nowhere is this more apparent than in the Indian adminstered Kashmir.[1]

The Indian Ministry of Home Affairs stated in its Annual Report for 2017-18, that since the start of militancy in 1990 and up to December 31, 2017, in India administered Kashmir 13976 civilians and 5123 security personnel were killed in various incidents. Separately, it confirmed that 21965 militants were killed from 1990 till March 31, 2017. However, human rights groups such as Jammu and Kashmir Coalition of Civil Society, put the number of civilian deaths from 1990 at a much higher figure at 100000. According to the UN, the Kashmir conflict "has robbed millions of their basic rights."[2] The reality on the ground in India administered Kashmir

---

[1] Kashmir Solution, www.fairobserver.com.

[2] Ibid.

is that India has deployed one soldier for every 12 Kashmiri (citizens of Jammu and Kashmir) an estimated 700000 security forces consisting of the army, paramilitary forces, Jammu and Kashmir police and other security agencies to fight 250-300 freedom fighters.[3]

Pakistan faces similar charges of human rights abuses in Pakistan administered Kashmir, ranging from political repression, electoral fraud, forced disappearances, torture and suppression of freedom of speech. Neither country has allowed the UN High Commissioner for human rights unconditional access to their respective protectorates.[4] Both India and Pakistan, first cousins and nuclear states, are currently in a quagmire, fluctuating between them depending on which government is in power, and particularly in Pakistan, how much the army chief or the head of the Inter Services Intelligence (ISI) exercises power over the civilian government. This is reflected in the armed forces' and intelligence services' approach, even if Pakistani and Indian civilians get along well.

It may be stated that the Kashmir issue is an intricate web that serves the interests of all in power and that nobody is actually interested in a permanent negotiated solution in which they compromise on their stated positions. Religious radicalization, nationalism and territorial ambitions have together created a blood-bath in Kashmir.[5]

Pakistan has been described by academics as an 'ideological state' that is"persistently revisionist" seeking to acquire territories in Kashmir that it does not need for security reasons, and also to reverse India's emergence as a global power. The army dominates its foreign and domestic policies and projects its conflict with India in civilizational terms in a face off between "Muslim Pakistan" and a "Hindu" enemy, with itself as Pakistan's saviour. It has

---

[3] Ibid.

[4] Ibid

[5] Kashmir Solution, www.fairobserver.com.

undermined efforts by civilian governments to normalize relationships with India, including through trade and investment.[6]

Further, complications occur because of the considerable hold that Pakistan's army has over the country's economy. The army controls one third of all heavy manufacturing in the country and upto 7% private assets. The Pakistan armed forces run over 50 commercial entities worth over $250 billion. Key appointments and public sector posts normally occupied by civilians are given to senior retired and serving military officers. With this size, scale and power, it needs a constant enemy to define itself in relation to. This complicates problems because India's traditional approach is to talk to the civilian government on the issue of Kashmir, whereas the army and the ISI - and even Islamists - run parallel governments in Pakistan. If the government of India is not talking to all the relevant people at the same time, then it is not simply talking to the correct people, and the peace process will ultimately be derailed.[7]

It is also important to look at the demographics in India to understand the overall context for a peaceful coexistence between its Hindu majority (80%) and Muslim minority (14%). In history, Islamic fundamentalists have been driven by an ideology of hatred and the desire to convert "other". However, India's Hindus have resisted conversion through 800 years of Muslim rule. Moreover, the bulk of conversions to Islam in India happened in the hinterlands (and not around the capital cities of the Muslim Sultans) as a result of the secular Sufi movement that Islamic fundamentalists denounce. Kashmir was historically a land of Sufi Islam Sufism suited Indians especially among the Hindu majority India because of its focus on love and humanity. Mainstream Islam, on the other hand, will find itself in perpetual conflict with a nationalistic and determined Hindu population, particularly in the hinterlands.[8] This fact needs to be accepted by the institutions in Pakistan, and respected in order to have any long term peaceful

[6] Ibid.
[7] Ibid.
[8] Kashmir Solution, www.fairobserver.com.

solution in Kashmir and also to manage its relations with India. In the words of a Kashmiri, "From 1947 to AK 47", which explains the transformation, India has also been following this transformation and expecting different results. Pakistan is no different. Its support for cross border terrorist attacks in India via proxies have effectively labelled the Kashmiri freedom struggle as a terrorist movement and caused them to lose western support. People on both sides of the border suffer from fatigue with their government's approach to Kashmir. Ordinary civilians in both countries are sick of powerful politicians and generals talking big on nationalism and painting the other as the enemy.[9]

However, the people are now beginning to understand the falsity of the above statement especially those civilians who interact with people across the border. Besides the issue of human rights violations, the amount of money wasted on the armed forces of both countries, the energy spent by their leaders on developing strategy and and policy to counter the other, the misuse of the issue to whip up fear and animosity before elections - all these could be avoided if the institutions were more sincere about dealing with the issue through negotiations. They need to focus on their growing economies and eradicating poverty both in Kashmir and more broadly within the two countries. It is important to underscore that India is less of a country and more a subcontinent where diverse people coexist as do multiple religions. Its diversity us both its strength and weakness because there have been various separartist movements against the Union at different points of time. Realistically what the Kashmiri people need to expect as an end goal is a solution within the status quo and a return of peace and prosperity to the two Kashmirs.[10]

Again, since 1989, the Kashmir problem has become intimately linked to the larger question of war and peace in South Asia. In looking at strategies for achieving solutions we need something that allows for parallel processing of the many issues, disputes and tangles that make up the Kashmir problem. Certainly it will

[9] Ibid.
[10] Ibid.

protect the vital interests of India and Pakistan, certainly it will recognize the ambitions and legitimate interests of the valley Muslims. But a just solution will also acknowledge the interests of others Kashmiris, not least the tens and thousands of Hindu and Muslim refugees, who fled the valley in fear, and the ethnically quite different Muslim population in Azad Kashmir, that has its own grievances with the Government of Pakistan. Indeed, a situation in which the refugees returned and again lived in harmony and under democratic norms could be defined as an acceptable solution.[11]

As Lewis Carroll suggested that if one did not know where one was going, any road would take one there. So we should begin to move down several paths at once and see which one lead to the solution when we do not ourselves the right path to our goal. Some will be clear right to the end and on others there would be obstacles. Certainly, it is better to find out the obstacles sooner rather than later.[12] Therefore, let us now find out the options regarding solution to the problem of the Kashmir valley which has been plaguing the subcontinent for years and look forward to implementing them, whereby India and Pakistan stop firing at each other, and let Kashmir live in peace while both countries add value and levy taxes in their respective adminstered Kashmirs. This requires letting go of the past and moving forward in a spirit of cooperation and mutual respect focussing on the future rather than being held by the past.[13]

First, The Kashmir issue needs an outside perspective because Indian and Pakistani strategists are locked in a mindless competition over tactical advantage and scoring diplomatic points. There is little strategic thinking about Kashmir. No one is looking beyond the immediate events and short term calculations of gain and pain. A solution cannot occur until it is supported by both states. and by Kashmiris of several varieties - but in the meantime it is important to have a place or an institution, where ideas,

[11] Stephen P. Cohen-Kashmir: Roads Ahead, www.brookings.edu.

[12] Ibid.

[13] Kashmir Solution, www.fairobserver.com.

possibilities, pressures can be focused. There needs to be a helping hand, a facilitator with no direct interest in the Kashmir conflict, yet with its resolution. Washington and Moscow each expertise and interests in Kashmir and neither is likely to make a high priority item.[16] However, the United Nations is already engaged in Kashmir. Its role is sanctioned by numerous Security Council Resolutions and it maintains a peace keeping presence along the ceasefire line. An expanded UN peacekeeping force or trusteeship is premature and would not have the support of at least one major party, India. Nor could such a force be imposed on India. But a UN personage that coordinates and consolidates various diplomatic efforts might in near future bear fruits.[14]

Secondly, nowhere in the Constitution of India, the term 'federal' appears physical. But India already has a hierarchy of federalism and Kashmir itself is the biggest variation. It has its own constitutional status in the form of Article 370.[15] Many suggested that India should now head into the position it has got anyway *i.e.* greater autonomy for Jammu and Kashmir. Within Jammu and Kashmir, there will have to be a further differentiation between those regions wating to become autonomous and those wanting to remain as union territory. The same process should be undertaken by Pakistan. Ideally, as some would suggest that looser loser federation of the two parts of Kashmir with their respective states, along with increased flow of people and goods between them would create a 'soft frontier' where both the physical and cultural boundaries between them were somewhat fuzzy.[16]

Thirdly, in the past high principle divided India and Pakistan as far as Kashmir was concerned. Pakistanis argued that India's control over most of the state violated the right of self determination of Kashmiris. India argued that Pakistan more often than not a a military dictatorship, was hardly a credible advocate of democracy. Pakistan's position ignored the agreed-upon basis for the division of British India and Indians could not bring

---

[14] Stephen P. Cohen-Kashmir: Roads Ahead, www.brookings.edu.
[15] Ibid.
[16] Stephen P. Cohen-Kashmir: Roads Ahead. www.brookings.edu.

themselves to recognize Pakistan as a democracy. But this change in Pakistan is important. It suggests a principle that both states should accept. This principle is that legitimacy will only flow from the ballot box, not gun. Both in the past have argued that voice of the people should be respected in Pakistan in Kashmir and India in Hyderabad. Both of them taken the opposite position when necessary and have used force. But forty odd years of preaching one principle and acting upon another have led to no where.[17] Both India and Pakistan should want to settle Kashmir problem with the Kashmiris who share their own commitment to democracy - a commitment that must include the protection of rights of the minorities. Getting agreement on this principle keeps open the door to a wide range of future relations between India, Pakistan and Kashmiris. It would ensure the future would rest on the consent of the governed, not the coercion of the gun.[18]

As desirable as it is to help India and Pakistan move towards agreement on democratic principles as a way to solve the Kashmir problem, it should be borne in mind that another principle would continue to divide them. New Delhi is not likely to give up the belief that its secularism would be damaged and that millions of Indian Muslims would be put at risk if a settlement of Kashmir took place on the basis of religion. The argument deserves serious consideration. It cannot be simply dismissed by Pakistanis as blackmail. Pakistan must think of ways they can reassure India that a change in the status of Kashmir (or parts of the state) would not be seen as acceptance of the two nation theory; India should likewise think of a way of peacefully accommodating Pakistani sensibilities and Kashmiri demands.[19]

The Kashmir crisis has deep historical roots. Particularly disturbing are those elements of the crisis that stem from Imperial conflict of the 19th century. The British acquired Kashmir but did not make it a part of British India; they established a boundary with China (and with the Afghans), but the boundaries were never

[17] Ibid.
[18] Ibid.
[19] Stephen P Cohen-Kashmir: Roads Ahead, www.brookings.edu.

demarcated. It seems absurd that two billion people should be entangled by conflicts generated by imperial governments that no longer exist. There are still border disputes apart from Kashmir. In Kashmir itself the line of actual control was never determined, which provided the opportunity for a bizarre struggle over the Siachen Glacier.[20]

None of these border or territorial are strategically vital; all could be settled tomorrow without any loss of sovereignty or national identity. None involve significant domestic population or ethnic rivalries. While these are not central to the Kashmir problem, they are related to it. This prudence suggests that all of the concerned parties take more seriously the negotiations already underway to resolve the India-Pakistan and India-China border disputes. In the long run, it would be important to associate the Kashmiris themselves with such negotiations and thus might be one inducement for them to help restore order within their own state.[21]

Again, both sides should stop relying upon what could be termed the alphabet diplomats and begin to constrain their self-deceiving disinformation campaign. Alphabet diplomats are RAW, ISU, KGB, KHAD, CIA and so forth and the local intelligence services have created a bizarre dimension to the Kashmir problem; supposedly well informed people of both the countries makes all kinds of wrong assumptions about which side is doing what to the order. Indians menacingly suggest if Pakistani Intelligence does not stop arming Kashmiris, "There will be hell to pay in Sindh." Pakistanis themselves cannot figure out whether Sindh is their Kashmir or is being stoked by the Indians. They claim that their dabbling in Kashmir is not the cause of India's problems but only the opportune exploitation by them. Next, we need to get the engagement model right. There needs to be time bound engagement on both sides with multiple stakeholders, including the civilian government, army, intelligence?, separatist leaders and civil society. This needs to include the resettlement of Kashmiri Pandits in the valley and

---

[20] Ibid.

[21] Ibid.

a cessation of Islamic fundamentalist activities and disarmament.[22]

Over 100, 000 Kashmiri Pandits fled the violence on India administered Kashmir in the 1990s. Currently, the numbers in India are around 62000; 40000 of them live in Jammu, 20000 live in Delhi and its satellite cities.[23] Kashmir traditionally has a peaceful culture called Kashmiriyat, signifying the centuries old indigenous secularism of Kashmir that demanded religious and social harmony and brotherhood. This needs to be restored to the valley. Interestingly, the Muslims in the valley wanted the return of the Pandits back and not in segregated townships. While the ghettos are undesirable in the long term, for reasons of security it is likely that initially a mix of new townships and restoring Pandits to the areas orginally inhabited by them is needed.[24]

The powers and constraints placed on the armed forces need review and modification. India needs to address the humanitarian concern around Kashmir by repealing the Armed Forces Act (Special Powers) units current form replacing it with a version that recognizes and protects human rights of innocent Kashmiris. This is unlikely to offer protection to known terrorists, putting a brake on enforced disappearances of innocent civilians detained for questioning.[25] However, it also means that new legislation is likely to bring in stronger military and criminal measures to protect the rights of the Indian Security Forces who have had to face stone pelting, to bring the stone throwers in line with law. The consequences of stone pelting should be made clear to the civilian population in advance so that if they indulge in this, it would be at their risk and responsibility. It is also good to involve the parents to control their underage children inadvertently becoming casualties. This should be part of civilian outreach and is absolutely essential to the long term success of any peace agreement.[26]

---

[22] Ibid.
[23] Kashmir Solution, www.fairobserver.com.
[24] Ibid.
[25] Ibid.
[26] Ibid.

India and Pakistan need to issue a joint person of Kashmiri origin card, a 25 year multiple entry Visa entitling Kashmiris (from Greater Jammu and Kashmir) to travel for upto 180 days and invest anywhere in Jammu and Kashmir, whether in Pakistan or in India. Controls can be there initially for periodic reporting to the local police stations every 15 days. But this can be dropped if the plan becomes a success and peace is restored. Moreover, where a Kashmiri is selling and buying goods from another Kashmiri across the border it can be agreed that there would be zero import duties and but other customs check on nature of the goods would continue as normal. A minimum curriculum for madrassa students including secular preachings of Sufi Islam should be taken up by the Government in schools.

India's Kashmir currently enjoys a high degree of autonomy on paper through Article 370 of the Indian constitution (except for Defense, Foreign Affairs, Finance and Communications) and Pakistan administered Kashmir also has significant autonomy, although actual practice differs in both parts. Specifically, it needs to be examined whether a higher degree of financial autonomy is required for both Kashmirs and how this would work.[27] It is currently unclear whether Article 370 can be legally dropped altogether or not. Irrespective of that India would want at least limited property rights, such as 99 year leasehold in India's Kashmir. Pakistan should do the same on its side. This also helps in national integration with mainstream Indians and Pakstanis.[28]

Personal and religious freedom must be protected in both parts of Kashmir. India and Pakistan need to create a joint mechanism that agrees a common minimum plan for the entire Kashmir area including, for example, enhanced monitoring if radical preachers of mosques and madrassas, including publications distributed by them.

A minimum curriculum for madrassa students including the secular teachings of Sugi Islam on love and humanity should be

[27] Kashmir Solutions, www.fairobserver.com.

[28] Ibid.

introduced and limitations placed on sharia courts to provide non binding arbitration and mediation judgment on civil matters related to Kashmir you family disputes such as inheritance, or divorce cases, review of fatwas issued on religious matters to ensure that they do not infringe upon the rights of individuals guaranteed under law, training for judges is needed and or blocked to curb radicalization as well as clamp down on the sale and distribution of extremist DVDs. Hawala funding needs to be monitored including the use of cryptocurrencies on the dark web. Exchange of intelligence information as well as joint security operations must be undertaken across both sides of the border to flush out any remnant terrorist pocket across the state.[29]

Eventually demilitarization is needed. This can be considered on other sides of Kashmir based on a phased approach once peace is firmly established leaving sufficient armed forces to maintain law and order and counter terrorism on both sides of the border.[30]

India and Pakistan need to come out with a plan to invest in Kashmir's industry, agriculture, services and tourism. There needs to be a budget and a new joint development body to execute these plans through both direct infrastructure investment, building institutions (such as popularizing high yielding agriculture) and lending via existing banks. It should be the same integrated plan with each country's money being spent on their respective areas. Of course, the Central Government should recover this money through taxes. The free ride to Kashmir has to stop in order to deal with the resentment that non Kashmiris have for their tax money being used in mollycoddling Kashmiris who enjoy autonomy unlike most other states.[31] However, it may sound preposterous but after the situation gets settled then the governments could think about it.

The Line of Control needs to be permanent in the context of the above which was in fact mooted by President Pervez Musharraf

[29] Ibid.
[30] Ibid.
[31] Kashmir Solution, www.fairobserver.com.

in 2002 at the Agra Summit with the Indian Prime Minister Atal Behari Vajpayee. This LOC will include the territory under Chinese control, legitimizing status quo and ideally solving India's other border disputes on its Northeastern border with China in the same deal. India would need to make peace with China on its Belt and Road initiative running through Kashmir, using it to benefit its half of Kashmir and the rest of India economically.[32]

It is to be mentioned here the full list of disputed territory in the area includes Jammu and Kashmir (also Ladakh), administered by India and claimed by Pakistan; Azad Kashmir - Pakistan and claimed by India; Northern Areas (Gilgit- Baltistan) part of Kashmir administered by Pakistan and claimed by India; Siachen Glacier, administered by India and claimed by Pakistan; Aksai Chin administered by China and claimed by India (India's 1962 War with China was fought here); and the Shaksam Valley administered by China and claimed by India.[33]

In the context of an agreement between India, Pakistan and Kashmiri leaders and separatists, unconditional access needs to be given to the office of the UN high commissioner for human rights on both sides of the new international border. Both countries need to act on any recommendations from the UN Commissioner, wherever possible. Jammu and Kashmir has hitherto been treated as a bilateral issue under the Simla Agreement of 1972, although this only referred to the process of building a political solution.[34]

Within Kashmir engaging with the civilian population to get their buy-in for the peace agreement and to help them alleviate their grievances is absolutely essential. A sustained campaign is needed, not a one-off effort and to work it needs to be well thought through (involving social psychologists) and well managed. Beyond Kashmir, an economically resurgent India also has a role to help eradicate poverty in South Asia. Hence, a similar 25 year multiple entry visa needs to be issued to prominent businessmen and persons (artists, writers, musicians etc.) in both countries to cover

[32] Ibid.
[33] Ibid.
[34] Ibid.

travel, investment, trade (part of, but not a solution in itself) and working anywhere in India and Pakistan. Automated immigration services could be set up in key cities.[35]

Pakistan would need to give up its "bleed India with a thousand cuts" policy using proxies and India would need to stop interfering in Balochistan altogether. Both would need to release all political prisoners from their respective jails. Pakistan would need to remove extreme messages inciting religious hatred against Hindus from all school text books and cease all training camps for Kashmiri freedom fighters.[36]

Both India and Pakistan are notorious for their shoddy implementation of otherwise good ideas. What is needed is a systematic approach with a jointly appointed team consisting of professional managers, members of the civilian government, army and intelligence, with proper authorities responsible and transparent discussion of policies, identifying all the changes needed and rolling them systematically. It also needs a high level project governance committee consisting of the respective Prime Ministers, heads of two parts of Kashmir, key central government ministers and army and intelligence chiefs meeting once a month to monitor progress.[37]

Having discussed the above it doesn't mean showing leniency towards the terrorists. Specific house to house searches based on information or combing operations should continue along with laser guided walls, electronic surveillance systems and drone surveys should be done to thwart or control as well as to flush out the terrorists to teach the adversaries a lesson. Along with this communication with the masses or to reach out to them would make the face of the army more humanitarian.

It is to be remembered that the solution is as simple as we want to be or as complex as we want it to be. But certainly without recognizing the existence of multiple stakeholders and having a

[35] Kashmir Solution, www.fairobserver.com.
[36] Ibid.
[37] Ibid.

time bound negotiation, we can never expect to see peace in Kashmir or in the region as a whole. India's approach of closing the porous border and treating Kashmir as a security problem is a short term stop gap solution that does not recognize the humanitarian cost nor does it treat Kashmir as the unfinished business of Partition.[38]

Pakistan's approach of funding cross-border fighters is a piecemeal and failing strategy that achieves nothing long term other than trouble for the local Kashmiri population. It remains to be seen whether both countries have the political will, wisdom and compassion needed for an actual solution. Thoughts words and deeds have to come together for this.[39]

An outsider is at a loss to determine what is fact and what is fiction. But it is likely that the insiders do not what the truth is either. This has created an unstable state of affairs. Regional officials on both sides seemed to have a good grasp of the problem and dangers of escalation. Neither side wanted to go to war for the sake of a few Kashmiris. That is still probably true, although there is a measure of crisis weariness especially in India.[40] However, the chances of an all out war over Kashmir is smaller than what the Americans think, but it is greater than the South Asians could imagine. The latter has to remember that all of the earlier wars between the two countries were caused in one way or other by strategic calculations which turned out to be in error. With the existing levels of misinformation and disinformation it could happen again, even with sober, responsible leaders in charge on both sides.[41]

Ultimately, the land being fought over in Kashmir is not as important as the people and their right to peace, security and to enjoy fruits of development - to lead a normal life that we take for granted.[42]

---

[38] Kashmir Solution, www.fairobserver.com.
[39] Ibid.
[40] Ibid.
[41] Stephen P. Cohen-Kashmir: Roads Ahead, www.brookings.edu.
[42] Kashmir Solution, www.fairobserver.com.

9

ABROGATION OF ARTICLE 370 AND AFTERMATH

In Chapter III already mention has been made how the princely state of Jammu & Kashmir ultimately acceded to India and the roles played by its Raja Hari Singh, Indian Prime Minister Jawharlal Nehru and Sheikh Abdullah. Also it has been noted there how Article 370 and later on Article 35A came into being and the subsequent conferring of special status on Jammu and Kashmir. Again, assessing the ground situation after the driving out of the tribals who were sent by Pakistan, Nehru had a premonition of getting support from the Kashmiris if a plebiscite was held at that moment and then Article 370 and special status of Jammu and Kashmir would be rendered useless.[1]

However, Sheikh Abdullah fearing of losing his foothold among the masses decided to part with Nehru by demanding a separate state of Kashmir for the Kashmiriyats. This was regarded as secession to Nehru and subsequently Sheikh Abdullah was put into prison. But still due to his long time friendship Nehru decided to release the Sheikh with an ulterior motive of permanently solving the Kashmir problem with the support of Sheikh Abdullah. But once the dice is cast cannot be taken back. The separatist movement had already gathered momentum when the Sheikh was

[1] The Statesman, August, 2019.

imprisoned. So even after the release of the Sheikh, it was a way of no return for Sheikh Abdullah as he now spearheaded the movement.[2]

This incident had upset the plans of Nehru as he being confident of getting Sheikh's support had planned to abolish Article 370 through Jammu and Kashmir Parliament and call for a plebiscite. But the resumption of unrest and the subsequent rearrest of Sheikh Abdullah led to the dissolution of Jammu and Kashmir Parliament and along with it the fate of the plebiscite was also sealed. Nehru was now in a confused state of mind so much so that in 1964 at UN General Assembly session India's non permanent representative remarked that plebiscite was not possible in the near future. From then onwards Article 370 and the special status of Jammu and Kashmir remained a thorny issue for every Government at the centre.[3]

It is to the credit of Modi Government where angels fear to tread, this government showed the guts to abrogate Article 370 and withdraw special status of Jammu and Kashmir on 5th August 2019 when every previous government at the centre back tracked on this issue. It was decided that Jammu and Kashmir Parliament would be dissolved and Jammu and Kashmir would be bifurcated into two Union Territories - Ladakh and Jammu and Kashmir. Later on Jammu and Kashmir would have an assembly. Along with this, Article 35A which conferred special status on Jammu and Kashmir stands redundant. Also, the Dogra dynasty of which Karan Singh was inheritor and who once fought for the upholding of the dynastic rule in Jammu in the 1950s, their dynastic claim to Jammu also became nullified.[4]

The precaution for this was taken before hand since 28th July, 2019 and the decision was a top guarded secret. About 50,000 security personnel were sent to Jammu and Kashmir, all the vulnerable points were sealed, suspects were confined, and

---

[2] Ibid.

[3] Ananda Bazar Patrika, February, 2019.

[4] Ananda Bazar Patriika, August, 2019.

pilgrims, which went on a yatra to the Holy Cave of Amarnath were asked to return. All these were done as a precaution against any untoward incident.[5] And ultimately the day came on 5th August, 2019, when the country held its breath to watch the events unfurling.[6]

Let us now see why Article 370 and Article 35A are controversial?

According to Article 370, the centre could not interfere in Jammu and Kashmir's internal affairs except defence, foreign affairs, finance and communications affairs.[7]

Secondly, despite being a part of India, the Indian Parliament had no right to formulate any laws regarding Jammu and Kashmir. If a law had to be formulated then the centre would have to take hold of property there which is prohibited as per Article 35A. In this regard the Supreme Court was hearing a case, which is mentioned in Appendix I of this book.[8]

Moreover, Article 370 provided a separate flag for Jammu & Kashmir. Article 144 of the erstwhile constitution of Jammu and Kashmir stated that the flag of the state should be rectangular in 3:2 format. Its colour was red and originally dedicated to the blood of the martyrs of 13th July, 1931 demonstration, but later came to symbolize workers and labourers. In the middle of the Flag the white plough represented the peasants. Next to the staff, three vertical white stripes represented three regions of Jammu, Kashmir Valley and Ladakh.[9]

The flag had its origin in the events which took place on 13th July, 1931 in Srinagar. During the demonstration against the Dogra rulers led by Sheikh Abdullah, the police opened fire killing 21 people. The blood tainted shirt of one of the victims was hoisted

---

[5] The Statesman, August 2019.
[6] Ibid.
[7] Ananda Bazar Patrika, August, 2019.
[8] Appendix I of this book.
[9] Noorani, A. G.-Two Flags One State, 4th September, 2015

by the crowd hailing it as the flag of Kashmir. Hence, 13th July is known as Martyrs' Day and officially it is declared a holiday in Jammu & Kashmir.[10] On 12th July, 1939, the flag was adopted by the National Conference, a political party. On 7th June, 1952, a resolution was adopted by the Constituent Assembly of Jammu and Kashmir, making it the official the state flag.[11]

The constituent assembly of Jammu and Kashmir in force until August, 2019, made it mandatory to hoist the state flag alongside the national flag.[12] But the newly elected members of Bharatiya Janata Party refused to comply with it.[13]

The government of Jammu & Jashmir led by the then Chief Minister Mufti Mohammed Sayyeed then issued a circular making it compulsory to hoist the state flag along with the national flag on the offices stating that "The state flag has the same sanctity and position as the Union Flag has under the Indian Constitution and other statutory provisions." However, within 20 hours the state government withdrew this circular.[14]

In December, 2015, the Jammu and Kashmir High Court ordered the government of the state to hoist the state flag along with the national flag on official buildings and vehicles of Constitutional authorities. However, this decision was contested by the Bharatiya Janata Party and in January, 2016 Jammu and Kashmir High Court stayed their decision. Despite the stance of the BJP, ministers of its coalition partner PDP continued to use the state flag alongside the national flag in official meetings. The youth wing of the National Conference also launched a campaign encouraging people to use the state flag stating that the state flag of J&K did not undermine or take away the protocol or status of the national flag and was clearly provided for in the Constitution of Jammu and Kashmir.[15]

---

[10] Ibid.
[11] Ibid.
[12] The Hindu, 14th March, 2015
[13] Ibid.
[14] Ibid.
[15] The Hindu, 6th Hanuary 2016

Ultimately, on 5th August, 2019 following the removal of the region's special status through the abrogation of Article 370 of the Constitution of India.[16]

Moreover, due to Article 370, no financial emergency nor general emergency could be declared by the Centre on the state of Jammu and Kashmir.

Also, because of Article 370, Ranbir Penal Code *i.e.* Criminal Procedure Code was applicable only in Jammu and Kashmir instead of Indian Penal Code which is effective in rest of India.[17]

Ranbir Penal Code: It came into force in 1932. The code was introduced during the reign of Dogra Dynasty with Ranbir Singh as its ruler and hence the code was named after him. It was made on the lines of Indian Penal Code prepared by Thomas Babington Macaulay.[18]

Lastly, the tenure of the Assembly of Jammu and Kashmir was six years.[19]

Now, what is Article 35A?

First, by this provision the permanent residents of Jammu and Kashmir enjoyed special advantages. And who the permanent residents of Jammu and Kashmir could only be decided by the Jammu and Kashmir Assembly.

Secondly, as per the provisions under this Article only the permanent residents of Jammu and Kashmir as recognized by the Jammu and Kashmir Assembly had the sole rights to buy property in Jammu and Kashmir.

Thirdly, Nobody apart from the permanent residents of Jammu and Kashmir could apply for jobs there nor they had the right to vote in Jammu and Kashmir.

---

16 Ananda Bazar Patrika, 6th August, 2019

17 The Statesman, 6th August, 2019

18 Singh, Bhim-Bitter Realities of Political History of Jammu and Kashmir, Feb. 6, 2010

19 Ibid. Also details of Article 370 is given in Appendix II.

Fourthly, if any woman, who was a permanent resident of Jammu and Kashmir, married any outsider, would be deprived of her property rights so much so that even her successors could not claim it.[20]

Having discussed the above Articles, let us now see the meaning of abrogation of these two Articles.

It was proposed in the Parliament that except the first sub clause of Article 370, the whole Article along with Article 35A stood null and void. As a result the Constitution of India which was applicable in all parts of India except Jammu and Kashmir, now could be applied here as well, which meant that Jammu and Kashmir now became totally integrated with India.[21]

Again, as per Jammu and Kashmir Reorganization Bill introduced and passed in the Parliament on 5th August, 2019, Jammu and Kashmir and Ladakh became Union Territories. Jammu and Kashmir would have an Assembly but Ladakh would not be having any Assembly.[22] On the other hand, the abolition of Article 35A meant:

So far till now through the President's directive India's relation with Jammu and Kashmir was determined by virtue of Article 370. And also as per directive of the President that Article 35A was included in Article 370. The abrogation of Article 370 led to also led to the abolition of Article 35A. Further, according to Article 35A, in order to introduce Reorganization Bill of Jammu and Kashmir, it had to be approved by the Jammu and Kashmir Assembly. The abrogation cleared the path for reorganisation of Jammu and Kashmir. Along with this Clause 367 of Indian Constitution was amended. It stated how to interprete different clauses of the Constitution.[23]

---

[20] Ananda Bazar Patrika, 6th August, 2019

[21] The Statesman., 6th August, 2019

[22] Ibid.

[23] Ananda Bazar Patrika, 6th August, 1957.

After the dissolution of Jammu and Kashmir as a state and formation of two Union Territories, in the case of Union Territory of J & K, the law and order would remain in the hands of the Centre, who would have the power to impose financial emergency in Jammu and Kashmir. Besides, a new economic dimension would open up now.

Further, the women of Jammu and Kashmir now would be free from worrying over losing rights over property if they married of their choice.[24]

Moreover, the Union Territory of Jammu and Kashmir meant it would be having a new lieutenant governor and the maximum strength of its Assembly would be 107 seats which would be further enhanced to 114 after a delimitation exercise. The current effective strength of the Jammu and Kashmir Assembly is 87, including four seats falling in Ladakh region, which would now be a separate Union Territory without a legislature. Twenty four seats of the Assembly continued to remain vacant as they fell under Pakistan occupied Kashmir. The Bill further said that Lok Sabha would have five seats from the Union Territory of Jammu and Kashmir while Ladakh would have one seat. The Union Territory of Jammu and Kashmir might nominate two women if it was felt they were not adequately represented. The Union Territory of Ladakh would have Leh and Kargil districts. There should be a Council of Ministers in the successor Union Territory of Jammu and Kashmir comprising not more than ten per cent of the total number of members in the Legislative Assembly with the Chief Minister at the head to aid and advise the Lt. Governor.[25]

The 'Kashmir Problem' has always been a bilateral matter between Jammu and Kashmir and the people of New Delhi. The rest of India has been living with one set of policies *vis-a-vis* Jammu and Kashmir for the last seven decades and the results have been underwhelming. It is time now to change those policies. Just like the people of Jammu and Kashmir and Ladakh have a stake with

---

[24] Ibid.

[25] The Statesman, 6th August, 2019

rest of India, the rest of India too has a stake in the new Union Territories. There is virtually no institution of the Republic of India that does not include Jammu and Kashmir within its scope and jurisdiction.[26]

Again as far as the property rights of women of Jammu and Kashmir are concerned, Article 370 itself is gender neutral. But by virtue of Article 35A, the definition of 'permanent residents' in the J & K Constitution based on notifications of 1927 and 1932 during Dogra rule is thought to be discriminatory. The 1927 notification included an explanatory note stating, "The wife or a widow of the state subject ... shall acquire the status of her husband as state subject of the same class as her husband, so long as she resides in the state and does not leave the state for permanent residence outside the state."[27]

This was widely interpreted as suggesting that a woman from Jammu and Kashmir who marries outside the state would lose her status as a state subject. But in October, 2002, a single judge High Court Bench of Jammu and Kashmir held that the daughter of a permanent resident of the state would not lose her permanent resident status on marrying a non permanent resident and will enjoy all rights including property rights. But no rights were granted to her children. This gender bias has been challenged in the Supreme Court. But with the scrapping of Article 35A, this too has become history.[28]

Let us now turn back our clock to 1953 when both the Articles faced opposition. Although the word opposition is used here with the assumption that some of the stalwarts of the Indian Freedom Movement who were known for hardcore patriotism had opposed Article 35A and Article 370, but it is indeed surprising that they had actually supported the above mentioned Articles, indirectly or directly for the sake of India at least for the time being. The

[26] www.economictimes.com

[27] Ibid.

[28] www.newsclick.in-An Article by Subhas Ghatade, 11th August, 2019

first name that comes up in this context is Sardar Vallabh Bhai Patel, iron man of India at that time and a close aide of Nehru.

Documentary evidences showed that the then cabinet led by Jawharlal Nehru worked on mutual consultation on the Kashmir issue. Patel's biographer Sri Rajmohan Gandhi pointed out, 'Mahatma Gandhi, Ambedkar and Nehru formed a crucial triumvirate that agreed that independent India would not be a Hindu Rashtra but one that offered equal rights to all. After Gandhji's departure and until Patel's death, Patel and Nehru differed on several matters but not on some fundamentals.[29]

With the help of others like Ambedkar, Maulana Azad, Rajendra Prasad and Rajaji, they entrenched secularism and equality in the Constitution.' When India gained independence, the future of three princely states namely Hyderabad, Junagar and Kashmir remained unclear as far as their accession to India and Pakistan was concerned.[30]

Documents that have been declassified including Cabinet and defence comitttee meeting records have now shown how Nehru and Patel worked closely to handle these three estates.[31]

Apart from the external aspects of the Kashmir issue, on internal aspects too, "Nehru and Patel worked closely together despite their differing emphases." In fact, N.G. Ayyangar, a cabinet minister without portfolio and who was also a former Dewan of Kashmir and the first Prime Minister of Kashmir, Sheikh Abdullah and his senior colleagues actually conducted the negotiations for Kashmir for several months in 1949. No doubt, these negotiations were difficult but Nehru seldom took a step without Patel's concurrence.[32]

"When Ayyangar prepared a draft letter from Nehru to Abdullah summarizing the broad understanding they reached, he sent it to

[29] Ibid.
[30] Ibid.
[31] Ibid.
[32] www.newsclick.in, An Article by Subhas Gatade

Patel with a note, "Will you kindly let Jawharlalji know directly as to your approval of it? He will issue the letter to Sheikh Abdullah only after receiving your approval.[33] Besides, Patel played an important role in getting Jammu and Kashmir's special status under Article 370 which was then called Article 306 being cleared by the Indian Constituent Assembly.[34]

Again, as per documents available Shyama Prasad Mukherjee had initially accepted the inevitability of Article 370. In this context, the noted lawyer and Constitutional expert, A. G. Noorani's important book Article 370: A Constitutional History of Jammu and Kashmir, published by Oxford University Press in 2011, examined Shyama Prasad Mukherjee's initial consent to the Article, as "the late leader had suggested to first Prime Minister Jawharlal Nehru to put a time bound rider on Article 370 and to specify for how long it was being envisaged."[35]

Further, veteran journalist, Balraj Puri, his book, The Greater Kashmir, had written, "Shyama Prasad's prolonged triangular correspondence with Nehru and Sheikh Abdullah on the status of the State, ... is the most authentic evidence of his stand on this issue. In his letter dated 9th January, 1953 to both Nehru and Abdullah wrote, 'We would readily agree to treat the valley with Sheikh Abdullah as the head in any special manner and for such time as he would like but Jammu and Kashmir and Ladakh must be fully integrated with India."[36]

However, given the situation, especially the way Pakistan was trying to disrupt the unity and integrity of India as was feared by Sheikh Abdullah in his letter to Jawharlal Nehru in January, 1953, on 17th February, 1953 Shyama Prasad Mukherjee in his letter to Nehru suggested, "Both parties reiterate that unity of the state will be maintained and that the principle of autonomy will apply to the province of Jammu and also to Ladakh and Kashmir Valley.

---

[33] Ibid.

[34] Ibid.

[35] Ibid. Also, A. G. Noorani's Article 370: A Constitutional History of Jammu and Kashmir in an article by Subhas Gatade in www.newsclick.in

[36] Balraj Puri's Article The Greater Kashmir in www.newsclick.in

Implementation of the Delhi Agreement which granted special status to the State, will be made at the next session of the Jammu and Kashmir Constituent Assembly."[37]

However, Shyama Prasad Mukherjee believed that the Article 370 was acting as a deterrent for cultural unification of the country and that it was harmful to the country's integrity as explained by him in a letter to Nehru in 1953. That citizens of India would have to carry ID cards while in a part of the country was something that he thought unfair. To protest this unfair 'permit system', he went to Jammu and Kashmir, from where he was arrested for illegal intrusion. He died a detainee on June 23, 1953 under mysterious circumstances at the age of 51 years.[38] His death had cleared the way for Nehru to grant Jammu and Kashmir autonomy as per the Delhi Agreement of 1952.[39]

Now, the Government of India has taken a bold step and opened up a new avenue for many opportunities by scrapping Article 370 and Article 35A. But everything will depend crucially on how the security situation evolves. Everyone is now braced for how the street will react once the blanket of security gets lifted. For now there has been a pretty muted response from much of the international community. But if the situation blows up then the reaction from most of the important and influential countries will be intrusive and interfering. The only way this can be prevented is by preparing and equipping the security forces to handle crowds much better and with greater sensitivity. While the international community will maintain a studied silence on anti-terror operations, they will certainly be forced to pressure India to ease up on the crackdown and to take some political and diplomatic steps for the betterment of the situation. The spiral of violence also could give a fillip to international jihadist organizations like the Al Qaeda affiliates and ISIS inspired and linked groups. And of course Pakistan is always there prowling on India.[40]

---

[37] Balraj Puri's The Greater Kashmir in www.newsclick.in
[38] www.dnaindia.com
[39] www.newsclick.in, an article by Subhas Gatade.
[40] www.orfonline.org

Again if a sense of desperation and hopelessness occupies the mind space of the people, then the valley could descend into complete chaos with tactics of other war theatres like Syria, Afghanistan, Yemen, East Africa being replicated.[41]

Alongside, the government will need to work overtime to demonstrate by actions and not merely by statements that the new political and constitutional arrangements are for the benefit of the people of the erstwhile state. There needs to be engagement and political outreach which cuts across party lines. The economy activities need to be kickstarted and the government needs to facilitate private sector investments in partnership with local residents. Public private partnerships need to be encouraged and promoted. A lots need to be done very quickly to ensure that a visible change is brought in the lives of the people which makes them develop a stake and instills confidence them that what has been done for benefit is for their benefit.[42]

But none of these is easy. There are decades of suspicion that colour the perception of the people and this won't change overnight nor days nor months. But now that the government has taken the plunge, the only option for it is to land safely to deliver and fast. Otherwise things may take a different turn, as the detractors of this government within India and outside are lurking to pounce upon it.[43]

---

[41] www.orfonline.org
[42] Ibid
[43] Ibid

CONCLUSION

The history of Jammu and Kashmir can be stated back to some 3500 years ago when the legendary kings of the Mahabharata ruled though written records about Kashmir can be had from some 2000 years ago when Kalhana wrote the only historical document about Kashmir in his book Rajtarangini. But from a peace loving Hindu state the state witnessed transformation in the British period especially during the period of Dogra rule in the 1840s. The accession of Raja Hari Singh to the throne of Kashmir opened the pandoras box from which the Indian subcontinent could not escape. Post independence, the indecision of Raja Hari Singh and thereby his delay in giving consent to accession to India had given an opportunity to Pakistan to take the wind away from the sail of India. It is to be noted that Pakistan wanted Kashmir to join her by virtue of Muslim majority there and domination of Islam, while Raja Hari Singh because of his princely state wished to remain autonomous and India because of Jammu and Kashmir's past history and tradition wanted her to join the Indian dominion. However, the secessionist movement of Sheikh Abdullah and subsequent invasion of Kashmir by the Pakistani army in the guise of tribesmen forced Raja Hari Singh to change his mind in favour of accession to India. But the Pakistani intrusion and the prevailing circumstances influenced Nehru, the then Indian Prime Minister to refer the question of Kashmir to the U.N.O. with a pledge for plebiscite, although the subsequent transformation of the situation in Kashmir forced Nehru to change his decision and Kashmir is now in a stalemate.

The conflict in Kashmir is convoluted to say the least and begs the question as to why India and Pakistan continue to fight so ferociously over such a small piece of territory. Today currently three countries lay claim to various parts of Kashmir. India administers Jammu, the Kashmir valley, Ladakh and the Siachen Glacier; Pakistan administers Azad Kashmir and Gilgit-Baltistan; while China governs Demchok district, the Shaksgam Valley and Aksai Chin region.[1]

While Ladakh and Jammu want to remain with India, the Muslim majority Kashmir region wants independence. The desire for autonomy in different areas of Kashmir has led to repeated uprisings and independence movements. The most prominent is a violent insurgency against Indian rule in the Kashmir valley that began in 1989 and had continued in ebbs and flows over the past three decades.[2]

The conflict in Kashmir is not just between India and Pakistan but also between militant groups in the region seeking autonomy from India. These groups include Hizbul Mujahedeen, Jammu and Kashmir Liberation Front which seeks independence for Kashmir and Pakistan based on Lashkar-e-Taiba, a terroristic group with connections to Islamabad and the 2008 Mumbai attacks.[3]

The Kashmir valley has become a militarized zone, effectively occupied by Indian security forces. According to the United Nations, Indian soldiers have committed numerous human rights violations there including firing on protesters and denying due process to the people arrested. The UN also cites Pakistan's role in the violence in Kashmir. Its government supporting the movement for Kashmir's independence from India by providing material and moral support - this allegations Pakistan deny. Pakistan also tacitly supports the operation in Kashmir of non Kashmiri extremist group like Jaish-e-Mohammed.[4]

---

[1] Shawn Snow-Analysis: Why Kashmir Matters in The Diplomat, September 19, 2016.

[2] Chitralekha Zutsi-Kashmir Conflict, www.the conversation.com.

[3] Shawn Snow-Analysis: Why Kashmir Matters, The Diplomat.

[4] Chitralekha Zutsi-The Kashmir Conflict.

As a result, consecutive Indian governments have managed to write off unrest in the Kashmir valley as a byproduct of its territorial dispute with Pakistan. In doing so, India has avoided addressing the actual political grievances of the Indian Kashmiris. An entire generation of young Kashmiris has been raised during the 30 yr. insurgency, who are deeply alienated from India. Militant groups in the region tap into this discontent, recruiting young people to use violence in their quest for Kashmir's freedom.[5]

Again, the question is why Kashmir is so important to India, Pakistan and China?

The answer is the glaciers and the fresh water they provide to the region and to India. The glacial water that flows through Kashmir, provides water and electricity to billions of Indians. Pakistan also relies heavily on glacial water flowing from the region to prop up its agricultural sector.[6]

With a growing population and increased need for electricity India has looked into the region to develop more hydro facilities. Pakistan fears that India may divert water necessary for irrigation and use water as a weapon against Pakistan. Kashmir is thus a major national security issue for both nations, the control of which could pose an essential threat to the other.[7]

In 1960, India and Pakistan signed the Indus Water Treaty, brokered by the world bank. The agreement gave India, the control over the Beas, Ravi and Sutlej rivers and Pakistan control over the Indus, Chenab and Jhelum. Because all the rivers flowed through India, she was given special provisions for hydroelectricity development.[8]

Sounding further alarm bells, research indicates that global warming is causing record melting of Kashmir's glaciers, which provide fresh water to it. Himalayan glaciers have lost an estimated

5 Ibid.
6 Shawn Snow- Analysis: Why Kashmir Matters.
7 Ibid.
8 Chitralekha Zutshi-The Kashmir Conflict.

174 gigatons of water; the rapid melt of water has been responsible for severe flooding in both India and Pakistan. With rapidly receding glacial water India and Pakistan will face prolonged water crisis, stunting economic growth and dry river beds will impact the agricultural sector.[9]

Kashmir is geo strategically located and serves as the main source of water and power generation for both Pakistan and India. The control of the region creates a zero sum gain in which the control of the rivers and glacial water could pose an existential threat to the other.[10]

The abrogation of Article 370 would definitely put a stamp of confirmation regarding India's authority over Jammu and Kashmir as well as would open up new areas of investment in the region. New investment would mean new opportunities and once the economy would develop the antagonism of the Kashmiris would hopefully subside. Also in the post abrogation of Article 370, Pakistan would be worried about their part of Kashmir which might go in India's way to leash Pakistan.[10A]

However, having said these there are other things which have been discussed above cannot be settled bilaterally by India and Pakistan alone - even if the two countries were willing to work together to resolve their differences. This is because the conflict has many sides - India, Pakistan and five regions of Kashmir and numerous political organizations.[11]

Establishing peace in the region would require of both India and Pakistan to reconcile the multiple and sometimes conflicting aspirations of the diverse peoples of this region. Only when local aspirations are recognized, addressed and debated alongside India and Pakistan's nationalist and strategic goal will a durable permanent solution emerge to one of the world's longest-running conflicts.[12]

---

[9] Ibid

[10] Ibid.

[11] Ibid.

[12] Ibid.

APPENDIX-I

ARTICLE 35A

Article 35A is a provision incorporated in the Constitution giving the Jammu and Kashmir Legislature a cartel blanche to decide who all are 'permanent residents' of the state and confer on them special rights and privileges in public sector jobs, acquisition of property in the State, scholarships and other public aid and welfare. The provision mandates that no act of the legislature coming under it be challenged for violating the Constitution or any other law of the land.[1]

Article 35A was incorporated into the Constitution in 1954 by an order of the then President of India, Dr. Rajendra Prasad on the advice of the then Prime Minister of India Jawharlal Nehru and his cabinet. The controversial Constitution (Application to Jammu and Kashmir) Order of 1954 followed the 1952 Delhi Agreement entered into between Nehru and the then Prime Minister of Jammu and Kashmir, Sheikh Abdullah, which extended Indian citizenship to the "State subjects' of Jammu and Kashmir.[2]

The President Order was issued under Article 370 (1) (d) of the Constitution. This provision allows the President to make certain "exceptions and modifications" to the Constitution for the benefit

[1] The Hindu, 26th August, 2017.
[2] Ibid.

of the 'State subjects' of Jammu and Kashmir. So Article 35A was added to the Constitution as a testimony of the special consideration of the Indian Government accorded to the 'permanent residents' of Jammu and Kashmir.[3]

The Parliamentary route of law making was bypassed when the President incorporated Article 35A into the Constitution. Article 368 (i) of the Constitution empowers only the Parliament to amend the Constitution. A five judge bench of the Supreme Court of India in its March 1961 judgement in Puranlal Lakshanpal *vs.* The President of India discusses The President's powers under Article 370 to 'modify' the Constitution. Though the Court observes that the President may modify an existing provision in the Constitution under Article 370, the judgement is silent as to whether the President can, without the Parliament's knowledge, introduce a new article.[4]

A Writ Petition filed by a NGO, We the Citizens, challenges both the articles 35A and 370. It argues that four representatives of Kashmir was never accorded any special status in the Constitution. Article 370 was only a temporary provision to help bring normality in Jammu and Kashmir and strengthen democracy in the State, it contends. The Constitution makers did not intend Article 370 to be a tool to bring permanent amendments, like Article 35A, in the Constitution.[5]

The petition said that Article 35A is against "the very spirit of oneness of India" as it creates "a class within a class of Indian citizens". Restricting citizens from other states from getting employment or buying property within Jammu and Kashmir is a violation of fundamental rights under Articles 14, 19, and 21 of the Constitution.[6]

A second petition filed by Jammu and Kashmir native Charu Wali Khanna has challenged Article 35A for protecting certain

---

[3] Ibid.

[4] Ibid.

[5] The Hindu, 26th August, 2017.

[6] Ibid.

provisions of the Jammu and Kashmir Constitution, which restrict the basic right to property if a native woman marries a man not holding a permanent resident certificate.[7]

The then Attorney General K.K. Venugopal had called for a debate in the Supreme Court on the sensitive subject. Recently, a Supreme Court Bench, led by Justice Deepak Mishra, tagged the Khanna petition with the We The Citizens case, which has been referred to a three judge Bench. The Court has indicated that the validity of Articles 35A and 370 may ultimately be decided by a Constitution Bench.[8]

[7] Ibid.
[8] Ibid.

APPENDIX-II

ARTICLE 370

Article 370 of the Indian Constitution is an Article that gives autonomous status to the state of Jammu and Kashmir. The article is drafted in Part XXI of the Constitution: Temporary, Transitional and Special Provisions. The Constituent Assembly of Jammu and Kashmir, after its establishment, was empowered to recommend the articles of the Indian Constitution that should be applied to the state or to abrogate the Article 370 altogether. After the Jammu and Kashmir Constituent Assembly later created state's constitution and dissolved itself without recommending the abrogation of Article 37, the article was deemed to have become a permanent feature of the Indian Constitution.[1]

The state of Jammu and Kashmir's accession, like all other princely states, was on three matters: defences, foreign affairs and communications. The representatives to the Jammu and Kashmir Constituent Assembly requested that only those provisions of the Indian Constitution that corresponded to the original Instrument of Accession should be applied to the State.[2]

Accordingly Article 370 was incorporated into the Indian Constitution, which stipulated that the other articles of the Constitution that gave powers to the Central Government would

[1] The Times of India, 4th April, 2018.
[2] Ibid.

be applied to Jammu and Kashmir only with the concurrence of the State's Constituent Assembly. This was a "temporary provision" in that its applicability was intended to last till the formulation and adoption of the State's Constitution.[3]

However, state's Constituent Assembly dissolved itself on 25 January, 1957 without recommending either abrogation or amendment of the Article 370. Thus the Article has become a permanent feature of the Indian Constitution, as confirmed by various rulings of the Supreme Court of India and High Court of Jammu and Kashmir, the latest of which is in April, 2018.[4]

The Text of Article 370 is as follows:

Article 370 - The Temporary Provisions with respect to the State of Jammu and Kashmir.

1. Notwithstanding anything contained in this Constitution, -
   a. The provisions of Article 238 shall not apply now in relation to the State of Jammu and Kashmir
   b. The power of Parliament to make laws for the said state shall be limited to -
      i. Those matters in the Union List and the Concurrent List which, in consultation with the Government of the State, are declared by the President to correspond to matters specified in the Instrument of Accession governing the accession of the State to the Dominion of India as the matters in respect to which the Dominion Legislature may make Laws for the State; and
      ii. Such other matters in the said Lists as, with the concurrence the Government of the State.the President may by order specify. The Government of the State means the person for the time being recognized by the President on the recommendation of the Legislative Assembly of the State as the Sadr-I-Riyasat (now Governor) of Jammu and Kashmir, acting on the advice

[3] Ibid.
[4] Ibid.

of the Council of Ministers of the State for the time being in office.[5]

c. The provisions of Article 1 and of this Article shall apply in relation to that State;

d. Such of the other provisions of this Constitution shall apply in relation to that State subject to such exceptions and modifications as the President may by order specify: Provided that no such order which relates to the matters specified in the Instrument of Accession of the State referred to in the paragraph (i) of sub clause (b) shall be issued except in consultation with the Government of the State: Provided further that no such order which relates to matters other than those referred to in the last preceding proviso shall be issued except with the concurrence of that Government.[6]

2. In the concurrence of the Government of the State referred to in paragraph (ii) sub clause (b) of clause (1) or in the second provision to sub clause (d) of that clause be given before the Constituent Assembly for the purpose of framing the Constitution of the State is convened, it shall be placed before such Assembly for such decision as it may take thereon.[7]

3. Notwithstanding anything in the foregoing provisions of this article, the President may, by public Notification declare that cease to be operative or shall be operative only with such exceptions and modifications and from such date as he may specify. Provided that the recommendation of the Constituent Assembly of the State referred to in Clause (2) shall be necesssary before the President issues such a notification.[8]

   The clause 7 of the Instrument of Accession signed by the Maharaja declared that the state could not be compelled to accept any future constitution if although The state was within its rights to draft its own constitution and to amend or abrogate the Article 370 except in aaccordance with the terms of the Article.

---

[5] India Today, 18 August, 2014.
[6] The Hindu
[7] Ibid.
[8] Noorani (battle), 2011, pp. 1–2

Article 370 embodied six special provisions for Jammu and Kashmir.[9]

1. It exempted the State from the applicability of the Constitution of India. The State was allowed to have its own Constitution.
2. Central Legislative Powers over the state limited; at the time of training, to the three subjects.
3. Other constitutional powers of the Central Government could be extended to the State only with the concurrence of the State government.
4. 'Concurrence' was provisional. It had to be ratified by the State's Constituent Assembly.
5. The State government's authority to give 'concurrence' lasted only until the State Constituent Assembly was convened. Once the State Constituent Assembly finalized the scheme of disperse, no further or taxation can be analysed.
6. The Article 370 could be abrogated or amended only upon the recommendation of the State's Constituent Assembly ended upon the recommendation of the government.

The Presidential Order of 1952 was issued on 15th November, 1952 at the request of the State Government, it amended the Article 370 replacing the phrase "recognized by the President as the Maharaja of Jammu and Kashmir by recognized by the President on the recommendation of the Legislative Assembly of Jammu and Kashmir as thel 'sadr-i-riyasat". The amendment represented the abolition of monarchy.[10]

To be noted that the Constituent Assembly was elected in 1951 and convened on 31 October, 1951. The basic principles committee of the Jammu and Kashmir recommended the abolition of the monarchy which was unanimously approved by by he Assembly on 12th June, 1952. In the same month the Hindu dominated Jammu Praja Parishad subbmitted a memorandum to the Preident of India demanding full application of the Indian Constitution to the State.

[9] Noorani (Article), 2011, pp. 5-7.
[10] Dasgupta- Jammu and Kashmir, 2012, p. 187.

The Government of India summoned a delegation from Jammu and Kashmir in Delhi for discussions on the relations between the Centre and the State. After Discussions, the 1952 Delhi Agreement is reached.

The State's Prime Minister Sheikh Abdullah was slow to implement the provisions of the Delhi Agreement. However, in August, 1952, the State Constituent Assembly adopted a resolution abolishing the monarchy and the position by an Elected Head of State, called Sadr-I-riyasat.[11]

The Presidential Order of 1954, officially the Constitution (applicable to Jammu and Kashmir) order, 1954, came into force on 14 May, 1954, issued with the agreement of the State's Constituent Assembly, it was a comprehensive order seeking to implement the 1952 Delhi Agreement. In some respects, it went further than the Delhi Agreement.[12]

The provisions implementing the Delhi Agreement were:

1. The Indian Citizenship was extended to the 'permanent residents' of Jammu and Kashmir (formerly called 'state subjects'). Simultaneously, Article 35A was added to the Constitution, empowering the State Legislature to legislate on the privileges of the permanent residents with regard to immovable property, settlement in the State and employment.
2. The fundamental rights of the Indian Constitution were extended to the state. However, the State Legislature was empowered to legislate on preventive detention for the purpose of internal security. The State's land reform legislation (which acquired land without compensation) was also protected.
3. The jurisdiction of the Supreme Court of India was extended to the State.
4. The Central Government was given power to declare national emergency in the event of an external aggression. However,

[11] Ibid. pp. 196–198.
[12] Chowdhary-Politics of Identity and Separatism, 2015, p. 48.

it's power to do so for internal disturbances could be exercised with the concurrence of the State Government.

In addition, the following provisions which were not previously decided in the Delhi Agreement were also implemented:

1. The financial relations between the Centre and the State were placed on the same footing as the other States. The State's customs duties were abolished.
2. Decisions affecting the disposition of the State could be made by the Central Government, but only with the consent of the State Government.
3. There is a provision for separate flag for Jammu & Kashmir and enforcing of Ranbir Penal Code will be in force in Jammu and Kashmir region instead of Indian Penal Code.[13]

[13] Dasgupta- Jammu and Kashmir, 2012, pp. 198–200, 212. Also, Kumar-Constitutional and Legal Routes, 2005, pp. 97–98.

BIBLIOGRAPHY

A. SECONDARY SOURCES

Anarchism, Documentation of Liberation Ideas.

Bandopadhyay, Sekhar- From Plassey To Partition, Orient Blackswan Pgt. Ltd., New Delhi, 2014.

Bhambri, C. P.-Nehru And India's Foreign Policy, The Economic Times, March 13, 2012.

Biswas, S. M.- Sher-e-Bangla, A. K. Fazlul Huq (1906-47), Mohabodhi Society Publishing Pvt. Ltd., Kolkata, 2009.

Bose, Sumantra-Kashmir Conflict, Path To Peace, Harvard University Press, 2003.

Chandra, Satish-Parties And Politics In Mughal Court, Haranand Publications, 1959.

Chitkara, M. G.-Kashmir, LOC, APH Publishing House, 2003.

Chowdhury, Rekha-Jammu & Kashmir, Politics Of Identity And Separatism, Routledge, 2015.

Dasguta, Jyoti Bhusan- Jammu and Kashmir, Springer Publications, 2012.

De, Amalendu - Pakistan Prastab O Fazlul Huq (Bengali), Parul Prakashani Pvt. Ltd., Kolkata, 1990.

Khan, Waheeda-Kashmir Conflict, Springer Publications, 2015.

Jalal, Ayesha, Jinnah, The Sole Spokesman, Oxford University Press, 1994.

Jerath, Ashoka-The Dogra Legend, Art & Culture, Indus Publications, 1998.

Majumdar, R. C.-History of India, McMillan Publishers, 1946.

Mansergh, Nicholas-Transfer of Power, 1942-47, Her Majesty's Stationary Office, London, 1971.

Menon, V. P.- The Transfer of Power & The Story of Integration of The Indian States, Orient Longman, 1956.

Murshid, Tazeen M-The Sacred And The Secular, Bengal Muslim Discourses, 1871-1977, Oxford University Press, 1995.

Nehru, J. L.-Discovery of India, Penguin Publishers India, 1946.

Panikkar, K. M.-Gulab Singh, Martin Hopkinson Ltd., 1930.

Puri, Balraj - The Question of Accession, Orient Blackswan Pvt.Ltd., 2014.

Rahim, E. & Rahim, Joyce L (ed.).-Documents of The Raj, University Press Ltd., Dhaka, 1996.

Roy, Jayanta Kumar-India's Foreign Policy, 1947-2007, Routledge, New Delhi, 2011.

Sengupta, Sukharanjan - Bangasamhar Ebong (Bengali), Progressive Publisher, Kolkata, 1976.

Sinha, Jaswant-Jinnah And Partition, Rupa And Co., 2005.

Srivastava, A. L.-Mughal Empire, Shivalal Agarwal & Co., Agra, 1959.

Wolpert, Stanley-Jinnah, Oxford University Press, 2005.

Zutshi, Chitralekha-The Kashmir Conflict, Cambridge University Press, 2014.

B. PRIMARY SOURCES (DOCUMENTARY SOURCES)

Ananda Bazar Patrika

Business Standard

The Statesman

Times of India

The Hindu

The Shillong Times.

The Economic Times

C. ARTICLES AND INTERNET EDITION

A Brief History of Kashmir Conflict, The Telegraph, www.telegraph.co.uk.

Abuja, Rajesh-How Sheikh Abdullah's Note To Nehru Saved Kashmir, m.hindustantimes.

Ahmed, Rashid-A Peace Plan For India And Pakistan, The New York Times.

Asia, Journal of South Asian Studies.

August 9, 1953, Why Sheikh Abdullah Was Removed, Kashmir Life, Kashmirlife.net.

BBC News.com.

Bajoria, Jayshree-Solving The Kashmir Conundrum, Council On Foreign Relations.

Behera, Navnita Chadha-Kashmir Demystified, www.brookings.edu.

Benkin, Richard L.- What is moderate Islam? Lexington Books, Archived.

Chitkara, M. G.-Kashmir, LOC, APH Publishing House, Archived.

Cohen, Stephen P.-Kashmir: Road Ahead, www.brookings.edu.

Gupta, Bal K.-Forgotten Atrocities, Memoirs Of A Survivor of 1947, Partition of India, lulu.com.

Habibullah, Wajahat-The Kashmir Problem And Its Resolution, United States Institute For Peace.

Hassan, Khalid Wasim-History Revisited, Narratives on Political and Constitutional Changes in Kashmir, (1947-90), Bangalore, The Institute For Social And Economic Change.

Indus Water Treaty, All About the Distribution Pact between India and Pakistan, indiatoday.in

Jawaid, Azaan-Hari Singh, The last Dogra King, the print.com.

Kalhan's Rajtarangini.

Kumar, Asutosh-The Constutional And Legal Routes In Ranabir Samaddar (ed.), The Politics of Autonomy, Indian Experiences, Sage Publications, pp- 93-113.

Noorani, A. G.-Article 370: A Constitutional History of Jammu and Kashmir, Oxford University Press, www.oxforduniversity.com & also, Kashmir, Blunders of the Past, Frontline.the hindu.com.

Prakash, Ved- Terrorism In Northern India, Jammu and Kashmir, and the Punjab, Gyan Publishing House, Archived.

Roser Max & Ors. (ed.)-Terrorism, Our World In Data.

Sharma, Mihir Swarup-Kashmir's Troubled Future, www.orfonline.org.

Shimla Agreement, Documents, Ministry of External Affairs, www.mea.gov.in.

Snedden, Christopher Snedden-Understanding Kashmir and the Kashmiris, Oxford University Press; also, Kashmir, The Unwritten History, Harper Colins, India and "What Happened To Muslims in Jammu, Local Identity, "The Massacre of 1947", And "The Roots of Kashmir Problem", South Asian Studies.

Snow, Shawn-Why Kashmir Matters, The Diplomat.

Tashkent Agreement, Documents, Ministry of External Affairs, mea.gov.in.

The Solution To The Kashmir Problem, www.fairobserver.com.

The New Indian Express (Internet Edition).

Timeline: India-Pakistan Relations, www.aljazeera.com.

Wangchuk, Rinchen Norbuk- The Untold Story, www.betterindia.com.

26th October, 1947, Why Maharaja Hari Singh agreed to accede to India, www.mpsofinfia.co.

The Places Visited:

National Archives, New Delhi.

National Library, Kolkata.

National Library, Newspaper Section, Kolkata

Ramakrishna Mission Library, Golpark, Kolkata.

The Statesman House, Kolkata.
The Telegraph House, Kolkata.
Writer's Building, Archive Section, Kolkata.
University of Calcutta, Library.

Picture 1: Kashmir Valley

Picture 2: Artist's Impression of Hassan-Sabbah, The I[st] Terror Leader.

Picture 3: Cabinet Mission (1946)-Sur Patthick Lawrence (Right) & Mohammed Ali Jinnah (Left)

Picture 4: I[st] Indo-Pak War, 1947.

Picture 5: Maharaja Hari Singh (September 1895–26th April, 1961)

Picture 6: Delhi Agreement (1952): Sheikh Abdullah (Right) & Jawaharlal Nehru, Indian Prime Minister (Left)

Picture 7: 1972 Simla Agreement- Pakistan Prime Zulfiqar Ali Bhutto & Indian Prime Minister Mrs. Indira Gandhi

Picture 8: Agra Summit: Indian Prime Minister Atal Behari Vajpayee (Right) & Pakistan President Pervez Musharraf

Picture 9: Kashmir Violence

SUBJECT INDEX